Discovering Modern Horror Fiction
II

edited by Darrell Schweitzer

WILDSIDE PRESS
Berkeley Heights, NJ ▼ 1999

To Alan Rodgers,
who has encouraged my horrorific endeavors

WILDSIDE PRESS
Berkeley Heights, NJ ▼ 1999

CONTENTS

INTRODUCTION

Welcome to *Discovering Modern Horror Fiction II*, the second volume in a continuing series of explorations of the modern literary phenomenon known variously as "horror fiction," "dark fantasy," or "scary stuff."

Of course horror fiction is *not* just a modern phenomenon. It has existed since remotest antiquity, in a variety of cultures ranging from the ancient Roman Empire to medieval China. As printed fiction, short stories and novels, it has been with us in English since the middle of the 18th century, its peak periods being, roughly, 1764-1849 (Walpole's *The Castle of Otranto* to the death of Poe), 1893-1937 (Bierce's *Can Such Things Be?* to the death of Lovecraft), and 1967 (*Rosemary's Baby*) to the present; with, of course, continuous activity in between.

While "modern horror fiction" may be a clumsy term—the Gothic novelists of the 1790s were writing what was, to them, "modern" horror fiction—but until posterity supplies us with a better one it will have to do. It does represent something distinct. The field has taken a definite turn, since about World War II, toward domestic realism, bizarre psychology, non-traditional or modernistically refurbished supernaturalism, and (most recently) explicit sex and violence. Strikingly, it has become more popular than ever before, even (probably) superseding the great Gothic explosion in the wake of Mrs. Radcliffe and M.G. Lewis. Stephen King may well be the most popular story-teller of all time. Perhaps that won't pan out over a century, but as far as the number of books sold per unit time, he can't be beat.

But he isn't alone. As I remarked in the introduction to the first volume of this series, King has attracted so much attention, and inspired so many books already, that it is useful to think of the *Discovering Modern Horror* series as typical volumes of Stephen King criticism—only about everybody else.

The purpose of these essays, and this series, is to provide background for the interested reader. Hopefully, you will be led to much more of the fiction you enjoy. There is no uniform approach, in terms of critical doctrine. I have not insisted that every essay be structuralist, or Jungian, or biographical, or whatever. There is a use for such carefully orchestrated explorations of literature, but in a general symposium like this one, I think a multiplicity of viewpoints is more helpful.

I have merely insisted that all the articles be informative, factually correct, and entertaining—clearly written and free of the ferociously impenetrable prose some academic critics lapse into.

While the first volume of this series was extremely well received, some reviewers wondered what my organizing principle was. There you have it.

Happy (horrorific) discoveries!

—Darrell Schweitzer
July 1986

PETER STRAUB: FROM ACADEME TO SHADOWLAND
by Bernadette Bosky

In less than a decade, Peter Straub has established himself as one of the major, and most interesting, writers of supernatural fiction. Due in part to his background in literature outside the genre, Straub's work is notable for grace and sophistication in both style and structure. More importantly, though, in a field rife with cliché characters as well as cliché menaces, Straub's writing is based on a coherent examination of basic human experience, expressed with both the convincing texture of mimetic detail and the metaphorical denseness of poetry. The true source of terror in Straub's writing is that the supernatural element grows so very credibly out of the choices, fears, and (most frightening of all) hopes of the characters, but then establishes autonomy as something even more horrible.

Straub's background in academe is evident both in the literary qualities of his work and the use of some autobiographical elements in his novels, which gives a firm, realistic background for the supernatural events, although the events themselves are severely altered to be even worse.[1] Born in Milwaukee, Wisconsin, in 1943, Straub spent summers with relatives in the Norwegian rural area near Arcadia, Wisconsin, which appears in a somewhat more sinister form as the setting of Straub's *If You Could See Me Now.* He attended prep school in Milwaukee, which provided the basis of Carson School in his novel *Shadowland,* and received a Bachelor's degree in English from the University of Wisconsin and a Master's degree in Contemporary Literature from Columbia. He then taught English for three years before beginning work in 1969 at University College, Dublin, for a Ph.D. This background shows up in a number of places in Straub's work, especially the Don Wanderly and Alma Mobley portion of *Ghost Story.*

Although he never finished his doctorate, academe's loss was fiction's gain. It was while working on an unsatisfactory dissertation on D.H. Lawrence, like Miss Teagarden in *If You Could See Me Now,* that Straub began his professional writing. His first work was in poetry, including contributions in the leading literary magazine *Poetry* in 1970 and 1971, and a collection entitled *Open Air,* published by Irish University Press in 1972. (In 1983 Underwood-Miller issued a selection of Straub's poetry called *Leeson Park and Belsize Square,* including most of the material from *Poetry.*) This background in poetry is very important to Straub's later fiction, in the facility and felicity of language, use of imagery patterns, and examinations of states of mind through the objective correlatives of exterior settings. Straub specifically refers to his first work, *Marriages*, as "an attempt to write a 'poetic novel,'"[2] but to a certain extent this is true of all of his fiction, and of great importance to it.

Marriages, published in 1973, was begun during Straub's second year in Dublin. As he said in a 1981 interview, "I suddenly felt myself more or less 'invaded'—invaded by fiction. Walking down the street, I'd be flooded with sentences about characters in various situations."[3] Straub quit work on his doctorate, and began his true career. This first novel is a mainstream literary work, which Straub describes as, "sort of like that Renata Adler book, *Speedboat*, except that it was a little more coherent"; it does, however, have one scene with a pair of ghosts in it, which Straub now sees as a harbinger of things to come.[4] After beginning a novel called *Under Venus*, unpublished until 1984, Straub entered the specific field of horror literature with the novel *Julia*, published in 1975.

Straub was at that time living in England. Although he still considered himself a mainstream literary author, Straub was concerned that *Marriages* was not selling well and his financial state was bad. Carol Smith, later to become Straub's agent, suggested to Straub that he write a gothic novel, which would be more commercial. It was a fortunate suggestion. Straub had been entranced with horror stories as a child, especially enjoying the Modern Library collection *Great Tales of Terror and the Supernatural*. Moreover, the move into the horror genre has proved a highly successful one for Straub, financially as well as artistically.

Julia has a quite different feel to it than his subsequent genre novels. This is due not only to the London setting (all the following novels take place in the United States), but to a very understated and subjective approach to the horror—what Straub calls, "a kind of Henry James lesson: that to be good, books of this kind had to be ambiguous, modest, and restrained. They had to have good manners."[5] Like "The Turn of the Screw," *Julia* could be seen as a story of either haunting or madness; an epilogue has characters expounding the latter view, but the evidence is weighted heavily enough so that the former conclusion seems more likely to the reader. Some of the best writing in *Julia* is in descriptions of mental states which are supernormal though not supernatural, ranging from dissociation and repression to paranoid suspicion, mystical trance-state and euphoria. (In fact, at the end of the novel the title character is behaving with classic depressive symptoms, while her brother-in-law shows the classic signs of manic disorders.) The depiction of subjective states, usual and unusual, is a major strength of the novel.

4

In some ways *Julia* is a largely successful mimetic novel, with recognizable presentations of contemporary character types. In others, it is a gothic in the sense of a woman's romance as well as in the sense of supernatural horror. Julia is a rich American, independent yet hesitant, feeling especially fragile after a mental breakdown. While in some ways she is a thoroughly modern figure, "a capable young woman, living alone in Kensington (p. 41)," she is also a gothic heroine, who admits she married Magnus Lofting half because she feared him, and half because he reminded her of her father. As the name suggests, her husband is even more clearly a gothic figure, commanding in his "huge male authority (p. 7)," irresistible to women. His sister, Lily, states, "He has *command*. Sometimes I think that Magnus is not from this world at all, or that he is thousands of years old, preserved by some black magic (p. 31)." Mark, Magnus and Lily's adopted brother, is, as Straub commented in an interview, "a parody of young leftist intellectuals"[6]; he is also an effective supernatural figure, too vague to be a villain, but petty and weak enough to be dangerous. As a spiritualist says of him, "He wants to be filled, like a bottle (p. 63)."

There is also, in the novel, a frequent gothic air of strangeness and the grotesque. The implicit sexual oddness that lies at the heart of the gothic here becomes explicit, including the close, almost incestuous relationship between Magnus and Lily (the childhood language they invented, called "Durm," recalls the imaginary kingdoms of Angria and Gondal shared by the Bronte sisters as children). The Dickensian character of Mrs. Fludd (named for the Renaissance magician), or the elaborate grotesque of Julia's disgust and flight when she visits a mental hospital (pp. 146-147) are in no way supernatural, but add to the gothic feeling of the book.

The supernatural traditional to the gothic inheritance is basic to *Julia*, and even more obvious than the other gothic elements: Julia's purchase of a large house, the first one she is shown, on an impulse that is almost a compulsion; the unsettling apparitions of a young blonde girl and her even younger Negro playmate; Julia's bad dreams. The manifestations of the haunted house run from the very traditional (noises, items broken) to the more contemporary (heaters which will not turn off, a "viscous brown jelly" (p. 172) from the tap instead of water). *Julia* is certainly closest of any of Straub's novels to the classic Anglo-American ghost story. Even in the novel *Ghost Story*, Straub uses the inherited material in the service of something other than an individual haunting by one person; *Julia* is a much less inventive, and less skilled, but more pure application of the form.

Julia shows the beginning of themes which are vital to Straub's entire *oeuvre*: the malevolent persistence of forces from the past, and the unavoidable burden of guilt. When the reader first finds out that the Loftings' child, Kate, died from a parentally performed emergency tracheotomy, that seems reason enough for the haunting Julia experiences; but the influences of that act, and the implications of guilt acknowledged and unacknowledged, spread in ripples throughout the book. In the same house, a woman named Heather Rudge stabbed her daughter Olivia, in what Julia calls a "deadly rhyme" of the more benevolent but no less fatal stabbing of Kate (p. 242). This is a guilt which somehow takes on a power of its own, and "touches" and "soils" even Mark, who has been directly involved in no particular past crime (p. 281).

When Lily tells Julia that the key to the haunting is not in the past but in Julia's own "state of mind," that is correct too. All four major characters in the novel are caught in the constant process of separating themselves from reality, retreating into themselves. Magnus, Lily, and Mark are all driven by desire for Julia's inheritance; as Straub has said in an interview, "you gradually discover that their common denominator is greed."[7] While the other characters isolate themselves in their respective wishes for power, Julia retreats into her obsession with the past and her current abnormal state, which are inextricably connected. When Julia thinks that Magnus has "no connection with what mattered" because he is "merely in the present" (p. 123), she demonstrates her dangerous preoccupations, leading her further and further from the shared life of the community. This interior haunting is as perilous as any exterior one; moreover, in some ways it seems to be causing it, since her study of the past is constantly treated as a dangerous invitation to its greater power over her in the present.

In *If You Could See Me Now*, published in 1977, the supernatural element is much more unequivocal. For almost all of the book one wonders, as in *Julia*, whether a supernatural agency is at work or not, but the end, unlike that of *Julia*, is indisputably preternormal. Straub states that he actually wrote three or four endings, some supernatural and some not, but decided that mundane explanation would be unfair: "I'd been working off supernatural emotion all the way through the book, and if I just turned into Raymond Chandler at the end, it's a betrayal."[8]

The novel is narrated in the first person by Miles Teagarden—a "lecturer in literature," "an instructor of the last gasp" (pp. 17-18) in contemporary literature—who returns to his relatives in a small town in Wisconsin, ostensibly to finish his dissertation but perhaps more truly to keep his promise of a twenty-year reunion with his childhood sweetheart, Alison Greening. He is neurotic, unsettled, morbid, self-critical and dissatisfied, although he is well enough characterized to be sympathetic, and has the advantage and appeal of any narrator, no matter how unreliable. (Straub has said that he made Teagarden more sympathetic in revisions, "but maybe not enough."[9] Teagarden finds himself immediately unwelcome in town: in some ways, his education and stay in New York have changed him too much; in other ways, not enough. Moreover, a series of vicious sexual murders have begun in town, and he becomes a suspect.

Although the themes of guilt and retribution from the past are important in *Julia*, they are even more central and more developed in *If You Could See Me Now*. Teagarden states, "I have always been a person with an enormous excess of guilt. My true vocation is that of guilt expert" (p. 62). This guilt is both imagined and real. Along with his personal, existential burden, Teagarden has a past too well known to the town, including shoplifting and an incident while swimming with Alison Greening. The latter is fully explained only very late in the novel, creating not only one of the solvable mysteries in the plot, but also a foreboding air of unexplained dread.

Miles complains about the insularity and grudges of the small town, which will not let it forget his past. In an evocation of *The Scarlet Letter*, he asks, "Why should your old sins be permanently pinned to your jacket? For all to read aloud?" (p. 36). This is largely credible; however, as Julia did, he also damns himself by his own entrapment in the past. He begins stealing again, though hiding money by the register for payment; he brings up the sheriff's childhood nickname and an adolescent embarrassment of his cousin Duane's, which they would rather forget; and finally, he becomes a living embodiment of the incident at the quarry, which virtually everyone in the town has reasons to wish forgotten.

Alison Greening, who Rinn says is destined to be Miles' "snare (p. 6)," is an ambiguous figure, sometimes successfully and sometimes not. There is simply no way to reconcile Rinn's view of Alison as corrupt and dangerous, and Miles' view of her as a complicated but innocent child-woman; Alison Greening, the real teenager, never comes into focus. Ultimately, though, the real teenager is unimportant. When Miles says, "She means freedom to me. She means life," and Rinn replies, "She means death" (p. 146), both are right. Alison primarily exists as what Goethe called the eternal female principle—*ewig-weibliche*—and as such she embraces all these in her own inscrutable female being. (It is amusing that one of her favorite novels is H. Rider Haggard's *She* (p. 200), about another manifestation of the eternal feminine.) Like the creature behind the identity of Alma Mobley in *Ghost Story*, Alison represents femininity not necessarily as inferior or hateful, but as totally "other"—awesome, unaccountable, and uncontrollable.

Unlike Julia Lofting, Miles Teagarden does learn from his encounter with the supernatural. As Straub comments, Miles rejects shoplifting as a return to the adolescent, "ridiculous, guilty old pattern."[10] After he waits for Alison at the appointed time and she does not come, Miles realizes, "Whatever I was going to be, whenever I could think of becoming something I could call myself, I was going to be different" (p. 309). He knows he cannot return to the sterility academe holds for him; when he leaves town with Alison Updahl, a down-to-earth namesake of his childhood love, it is a sign of him accepting his nature, but re-making his past.

With his fourth published novel, Straub secured an undisputed place in the history of the genre; *Ghost Story*, published in 1979, is a work of both great polish and great inventiveness. As the title suggests, Straub wanted to incorporate as many classic elements of the genre as possible, ranging from werewolves and the vengeful dead to, Straub states, "the old codgers sitting around telling stories, which Stephen King tells me is the oldest cliché in the book."[11] The structural device of the tales-within-a-tale also allowed Straub full play of literary allusion, which is used exceedingly well. Originality and coherence also characterize the book, however, provided by the uncanny creatures that lurk behind the various mythical and literary masks, and by Don Wanderly and the people of Milburn, New York, as they encounter those creatures.

When Straub set out to use the traditional material of the form, he says, he took about six months to read and re-read the classics. Influences he has mentioned include Edgar Allan Poe, Ambrose Bierce, Edith Wharton's ghost stories, J. Sheridan Le Fanu, 19th century British novelist Mrs. Gaskell, H.P. Lovecraft and his circle, a number of Continental supernatural books, and of course Henry James (and probably M.R. James) and Nathaniel Hawthorne, who are acknowledged in the last names of two characters.[12] Straub also states that Arthur Machen's "The Great God Pan" was very much in his mind when writing *Ghost Story*.[13] That influence is probably most clear in the glimpse of the shape-shifting creature without its "mask" as it dies—a form so horrible that it was the probable cause of Edward Wanderly's heart attack (pp. 540-543).

A more recent influence was also crucial to *Ghost Story*, and to Straub's writing since then; Straub acknowledges a debt to Stephen King, both personally and professionally. Straub mentions that King's *Salem's Lot* was important as a lesson in structure, of both plot and setting, "without getting lost among a lot of minor characters."[14] Both novels and towns are very different, but Straub did benefit from the use of a number of techniques, including panoramic surveys of events in the town, some of which are not related to the horror and many of which (not always obviously at first) are. Straub combined this with explicit or implicit hints about future events—a development of the approach shown in the police "statements" in *If You Could See Me Now*—to excellent effect. The structural influence of *Salem's Lot* can also be seen in the frame-narratives of the two novels. Perhaps there is also an effect of the adopted father/son relationship of King's Ben Mears and Mark Petrie on Straub's Don Wanderly and Peter Barnes.

The most general and important King influence is the counterbalance he provided to Straub's earlier Jamesian, Britishly restrained tone; as Straub states, King showed him that horror novels could be, "bad mannered, noisy, and operatic,"[15] and be both stylish and effective. Some readers feel that in *Floating Dragon*, Straub has carried the tendency too far, erring on the side of pyrotechnics as *Julia* may be said to err on the side of understatement. In *Ghost Story* the balance between the two approaches is just about perfect, the literary subtlety and the visceral terror working together.

The human center of *Ghost Story* is the Chowder Society, which is, as the novel opens, a group of four old men who meet in formal dress to tell stories: Sears James, Ricky Hawthorne, Lewis Benedikt, and John Jaffrey. They are, as Stephen King notes, an essentially conservative force,[16] linked to the town first in their values and history, then in supernatural besiegement. The configuration of four characters tied together by the supernatural is a basic one for Straub, but *Ghost Story* provides an interesting turning-point in the reasons for the group bond. Julia and the three Lofting siblings are joined only by guilt, and Miles Teagarden points out in *If You Could See Me Now* that he, his cousin Duane, the sheriff, and Paul Kent are all single men, tied together by guilt and (or for) the past (p. 183).

The Chowder Society begins as the same kind of society of guilt: all were involved in the accidental killing of actress Eva Galli. After the deaths of two of their members, the remaining four continue to meet in part because they would be afraid not to (p. 324). But from then on, when a member is killed, he is replaced immediately by a new member not tied to the guilt of the past; Don Wanderley shows up literally at John Jaffrey's funeral (p. 159-160) and Peter Barnes' initiation is an encounter with the shapeshifter in which Lewis Benedikt is killed (p. 390). Wanderley and Barnes shift the focus of the group away from guilt—emphasizing the fellowship which was always there, but bringing the ability to oppose the evil on a more pure level. Peter, especially, who has not even had the encounter Wanderley had with the thing in the guise of Alma Mobley, is invaluable for his innocence; it is because of this as well as Peter's strength of will that Wanderley says, "if we get those things before they get us, it'll be mostly because of you" (p. 463).

The human center of the novel, the Chowder Society, is opposed to the non-human center: the creature or creatures variously known as shapeshifters, nightwatchers (Don Wanderley's book, *The Nightwatcher*, is probably a nod to Thomas Tessier's *The Nightwalker*), or the American Indian term manitou. Here the novelist shows his mastery of working variations on a theme, in an improvisatory way Straub thinks of as similar to the jazz music of which he is fond.[17] The fatally beautiful woman with the initials A.M.; the corrupt Gregory and Fenny Bate (or Benton) introduced in a story by Sears James which is reminiscent of "The Turn of the Screw," but with a hint of the werewolf or ghoul to them; the matron Florence de Peyser;

even the Jehovah's Witness and Dr. Rabbitfoot (which Straub states came from a real Witness and *Watchtower* title, synchronistically appearing at his door just as he needed a new motif)[18] —all of these appear and reappear in eerie variations, creating a certainty that there is one coherent force but an uncertainty as to who—or what—it could be.

Alma Mobley (note that the first name means "soul") in her various avatars is the depiction of a figure that lurks in virtually all of Straub's work, from his poetry forward. In *Ghost Story*, these function credibly as realistic characters as well as supernatural forces in a way that is not true in *If You Could See Me Now*; as a result, the writing is some of the strongest and best Straub has produced. All of the encounters with these figures, but especially the extended depiction of Don Wanderley in love with Alma Mobley, the graduate student from New Orleans, convincingly convey a sense of mystery, yet of very human appeal. The reader can feel the attraction of a woman who, as Don Wanderley describes her, "lived in perfect consonance with her femininity; ...she seemed ageless, even timeless, beautiful in a nearly hieratic and mythic way" (p. 213). Beyond that is the successful sense of the supernatural, trans-human, and almost inconceivable power of the manitou. This *is* the eternal feminine, and both the horror and the attraction are strikingly portrayed. When its taped voice tells the Chowder Society, "I will take you places you have never been" (p. 466), the reader not only believes it, but is half tempted to go there too.

Primarily, *Ghost Story* is a success in handling what Straub has repeatedly called "a larger canvas," in plot and setting as well as supernatural effects. The various sub-plots, both social and supernatural, help to establish Milburn and its residents as real people, but also to show the effects of the malignant presence spreading throughout the town. The device of structural echoes, developed in the first novels, becomes a major source of strength and coherence in *Ghost Story, Shadowland*, and *Floating Dragon*. Repetition of events, words or speech patterns, and images, "so the whole book is interconnected," as Straub states,[19] is accomplished both through the narrative voice and through the supernatural agency of the manitou.

Another device which is important in the earlier novels, but even better handled in *Ghost Story*, is the blending of subjective and objective experiences. "The other thing I like about *Ghost Story*," Straub states, "...are those passages in which the characters aren't sure what is real. They're pitchforked into something else and they have to grope around and try to figure out what is going on."[20] This becomes the central theme of *Shadowland*.

Straub had begun the novel before moving back to America from England in 1979, and it was published in 1980. In many ways, *Shadowland* is a great departure from the novels before it; it seems a

10

conscious attempt to develop something different. Straub has stated that he "steered clear of" the theme of guilt, sexual and historical, in the book[21]. Moreover, the representative of the feminine in *Shadowland*, Rose Armstrong, has the allure and strangeness of Alison Greening or Alma Mobley, but not the devouring force; in fact, she is fragile, with a wounded look that, "broadcast[s] vulnerability" (p. 242). (This may also be conscious, following a 1979 interview in which Gahan Wilson asked Straub what his problem with women was.)[22] *Shadowland* is understated and oblique, and some readers have found it unsatisfactory; it is also a strongly mythic and poetic book, and other readers feel it may be his best novel.

While a haunting lies at the heart of every other genre novel of Straub's, magic is the heart of *Shadowland*—both stage magic and supernatural magic. The first part of the novel takes place in a prep school in Arizona (the regional setting is disappointingly under-used compared to other Straub writing), where freshmen Tom Flanagan and Del Nightingale meet. Tom is interested in card tricks; Del spends the summers with his uncle Coleman Collings, a retired stage magician of some fame, who is teaching his nephew the trade. Both boys are hungry for stage magic, and perhaps for deeper magic as well. The rest of the book takes place at the uncle's estate, Shadowland, where the boys' realities increasingly grow both phantasmagoric and potentially deadly.

This novel is to some extent haunted by the past, also, but in a different way. Del explains that summers at Shadowland have always echoed what he had experienced, since, "That's all a part of magic—working with what's in your mind. Or on your mind" (p. 159). Thus all the events at Carson School somehow anticipate Shadowland, and all of the events in Shadowland show reflections (often distorted) of the events in the school. Like the appearances of the various shapeshifters in *Ghost Story*, this produces a feeling of the uncanny, with inexplicable events which, however, seem to be organized around an unstated order.

As *Ghost Story* is formed and developed around the Anglo-American supernatural tale, *Shadowland* reaches even further back to the European fairy tale. Versions of "The Little Goose Girl," taught in Tom and Del's English class, occur in *Shadowland*; primarily, Straub states that the feeling of Tom and Del lured to Shadowland and manipulated by Collins is essentially, "the atmosphere of Hansel and Gretel, of two children lost in a wood."[23] Straub does capture that menace well: *Shadowland*, though not a ghost story, is certainly a horror novel. Straub has a special challenge in the task of progressively revealing the evil of Collins and his ambition, since all the other characters are in various degrees either innocent, taken in by the magician's facade, or totally his creature (in some cases, perhaps literally). This is one weak point in the novel, since Straub does not always succeed; but as Tom and then Del accept the reality that their mentor is a wolf in mage's clothing, the reader feels the terror of that as well.

The other major influence on the novel is *The Magus*, by contemporary British author John Fowles. Despite Straub saying, "it wasn't that I wanted to imitate *The Magus*,"[24] the influence of that novel on the plot and structure of *Shadowland* is even greater that that of *Salem's Lot* on *Ghost Story*: the powerful patriarch and his estate, including a beautiful young woman inexplicably under his control and an old woman who does not speak English; living tableaux, enacted by the young woman and others, presenting myths (in *Shadowland*, fairy tales) and events from the man's past; the man's narration of a wartime event that changed his life entirely; and the confused visitor (for Fowles, a prep school instructor instead of two students) who is the object of all the reality play, finally reaching a new maturity because of it. However, Straub's use of his literary inheritance, here as in *Ghost Story*, is anything but derivative; the literary resonances deepen the texture of the writing, and in no way detract from the mimetic and emotional effects. In fact, in further blending the interior and material worlds, they heighten the affective appeal.

Shadowland is a flawed book in some ways, but what it does accomplish it does better than any other of Straub's novels. The character development is excellent, especially the depiction of Tom and Del, both in the school and at Shadowland, as two very real adolescent boys trying to become young men; their friendship, sometimes strained by Del's jealousy and Tom's feelings of betraying Del, is moving and realistic. The imagistic unity of the book is a step beyond that of *Ghost Story*; the use of bird imagery throughout the novel, for instance, would not be shamed by comparison to *Portrait of the Artist as a Young Man*. Most of all, however, the magic *feels* like magic. The primitive force of the fairy tales and the convincing descriptions of the inner and the outer becoming one give *Shadowland* a unique atmosphere.

Floating Dragon, published in 1983, in some ways shows new directions for Straub, while in others it is a return to the themes from which *Shadowland* was a departure. As *Ghost Story* is in a sense an omnibus of the literary roots of the genre, *Floating Dragon* is an omnibus of horrific devices and conventions, from bats and walking corpses to DRG-16, a gas any mad scientist would be proud to have developed. Straub throws in everything but the kitchen sink, and then throws in the kitchen sink. But it's a really *great* kitchen sink.

While writing *Floating Dragon*, Straub began collaboration with Stephen King on a supernatural epic (finished but not in print as of this article) called *The Talisman*. Straub has stated that the collaboration, and his "pleasure in some of its gaudier toys," is one reason for the flamboyance of his own novel.[25] King's influence may also appear in the interweaving of the various plot-threads in the novel, although the narrative development is much more stylish and sophisticated than King's, with various patterns of intercuts, hints of events past and future, and flashbacks and flashforwards, all handled with assurance and skill. Certainly *Floating Dragon* is the most impressively structured of Straub's novels, as much beyond *Ghost Story* as *Ghost Story* was beyond his earlier genre novels.

The two major thematic foci also continue the development of the earlier work; these are indicated by the two epigraphs of the book. A quotation from Frederick K. Price reads, "The devil is a dumb spirit. All the devil knows is what you tell him with your own big fat mouth." *Floating Dragon* is primarily concerned with the joining of objective and subjective perceptions, though in a different way from *Shadowland*; while it lacks the Shadowland eerieness, it more than makes up for it in pyrotechnics. Psi abilities in at least two of the characters, the hallucinogenic properties of the escaped gas, and the continued baleful presence of a supernatural being called the Dragon provide a number of distorting lenses through which reality is seen; moreover, some presumably objective effects, such as a series of violent murders or the "leakers," whose skin is turned to colloid by the gas, are as grotesque as any hallucination.

This is not as eerie as *Shadowland* because, while reality is constantly distorted, there is never the possibility, as there is in the other novel, that there may be no reality at all behind the appearances. The scene in which the police showing of *The Choir Boys* somehow ends up in a massacre (pp. 348 ff.) is the most Shadowland scene in *Floating Dragon*, and the strongest. Moreover, too many of the scenes in *Floating Dragon* substitute the horrors of the viscera for the terrors of the mind, or blend them clumsily. Perhaps the greatest weakness is that the cornucopia of genre images and devices makes it very difficult for Straub to maintain the kind of unity, or feeling of some unstated center, that is so important to both *Ghost Story* and *Shadowland*. There are a number of structural echoes, many of them quite skillfully done; but the sheer quantity of different images sometimes makes their pattern seem rickety and haphazard.

The other epigraph is from John Ashbery's *Haunted Landscape*: "Now time and the land/are identical,/Linked forever." In many ways, *Floating Dragon* is the best depiction Straub has done of a town haunted by its burden of guilt in the past. The colonial heritage of Hampstead, Connecticut, lives in the four protagonists, each descended from one of the families that settled it, and by their adversary, who came among those families as a man named Gideon Winter. Graham Williams, an elderly writer who is one of the four opposing the Dragon, states, "Whatever happened back then is affecting us now. Isn't that always true of history?" (p.185). Straub's development of the town's history is good, and vital; unlike the guilt in Straub's other novels, that in *Floating Dragon* is the entire town's, if it is anyone's.

13

Williams says that this is a case of something like demonic possession only if, "an entire stretch of seacoast can be possessed. Or can possess" (p. 192).

The embodied center of the town's evil is Gideon Winter, who plays a role analogous to that of the earlier female phantasms. Unfortunately, he is not as convincing a figure as Alma Mobley, or perhaps even Alison Greening, and is not always adequate to his purpose. Despite his apparently limitless powers, there is not the sense of the uncanny, the "other" that there is with the earlier characters. Moreover, despite a female historian's apparent attraction to his legend ("women all love a dragon," she tells Graham (p. 199)) and statements that his human incarnations have great sexual appeal, the reader is only told, never shown. The Dragon does not even have the sexual force of Magnus Lofting, let alone the haunting and realistic presence of Alma Mobley. Straub is probably right to try this new direction, but his handling of it in this book is unsatisfying.

The eternal feminine is present in *Floating Dragon*, however, in the climactic scene where Patsy McCloud psychically enfolds and energizes her three male companions in slaying the Dragon. This is the same unaccountable and awesome female force as in Straub's other novels, but here turned to help the men, as it is there turned against them: "It was like opening her body, her essence spilled out to each of them....They melted into her; this was unbearably strong, and the strength was hers" (p. 492). This is also a new kind of altered state of being for Straub's already broad repertoire; it is a healthy, mystical equivalent of Mark's pathological euphoria in *Julia*. The scene of Patsy's transfiguration is not totally successful, but like the magic of Shadowland it has a convincing feel to it. Similar, but even more successful, is the sense of communion the four feel after slaying the Dragon, a touch of goodness to which even onlookers react for a week or two after (pp. 507-508).

In fact, although by far the most gruesome of Straub's novels, *Floating Dragon* is also its brightest and most optimistic. Unlike the Chowder Society, the four heroes of *Floating Dragon* have no personal guilt, and are bound only by deep friendship and dedication to the task. There is also an active force for good in the novel, which makes it unique in Straub's writing. (The figure of Bud Copeland/Speckle John may be such a force in *Shadowland*, but it is clear that he is also a projection of Tom's own power (p. 448).) This is especially shown in the transformation of meager human weapons into glowing swords, which happens inexplicably in the presence of the Dragon and the loving will of his human antagonists. Straub may have been influenced here by a similar scene in *Salem's Lot*; certainly, what King says of the glow surrounding Mark's vampire-killing stake would apply to Straub's intervening force as well: "it was whatever moved the greatest wheels of the universe" (p.408).

14

Floating Dragon is Straub's most recent novel at the writing of this article. Although he does not write short stories—"They seem more like poems than novels, and I have a lot of trouble writing them."[26] Straub does have one published novella, "The General's Wife," which appeared in the May 1982 issue of *Twilight Zone* magazine and was issued that same year in a deluxe volume by Donald M. Grant, Publisher, Inc. In the introduction to the latter edition, Straub explains that the piece, inspired by Carlos Fuentes' novel *Aura*, was originally part of *Floating Dragon*, edited out for reasons of length and at the suggestion of his editor, Bill Thompson.[27]

The novella is very good, but its extirpation from the novel was definitely for the best. For one thing, the mood is totally different from the rest of novel; in fact, in some ways it is a return to the hints and understatement of Straub's Jamesian writing such as *Julia*. Except for the flies and blood of the final scene, and perhaps the appearance of cats (which could be a foreshadowing of the feline apparition in the novel), the imagery and events of "The General's Wife" have no continuity with the predominant patterns of *Floating Dragon*. Moreover, past involvement in an episode like this does not seem to fit with Patsy as she is depicted in the novel, somewhat shocked by the intrusion the supernatural evil (even though she knows she is psychic) and relatively innocent sexually.

The piece, with the characters' names changed, does stand very well on its own. It has an unusual, mythic feel to it; the events seem to parse out less well into a rational plot than those of Straub's novels, but perhaps for that reason the events and associations seem to be ordered by a more poetic correspondence of mood, image, and structure. Straub describes *Aura* as, "like seeing how Robert Aickman might have written if he'd been born in Mexico City,"[28] and "The General's Wife" might also be compared to that contemporary British writer's horror short stories. This tale of a young American woman hired to edit the military papers of an elderly recluse in London, and her involvement with his eerie grandson, is elliptically told, evocative although somewhat obscure.

It will be interesting to see where Straub's career takes him next. Certainly, his name—and market—is assured. *Ghost Story, Shadowland,* and *Floating Dragon* all have had impressive stays on the bestseller list. Two of his books have been made into movies: *The Haunting of Julia,* also known as *Full Circle,* was released in 1977, and *Ghost Story* appeared as a film in 1981. Moreover, Straub's literary background, and the way in which some of his writing functions as metafiction, seems likely to make Straub interesting to the critics despite the prejudice against genre writing. Straub states that he sees a yet-unpublished novel by King called *It,* their collaboration *The Talisman,* and his own *Floating Dragon* as "a kind of gigantic trilogy,"

15

dealing with many of the same concerns and stemming from the same impulses.[29] We can look forward to his future work with pleasure.

NOTES

1. All biographical information is from Jay Gregory, "TZ Interview: Peter Straub," *Twilight Zone Magazine,* May 1981, pp. 13-16; and Paul Gagne, "An Interview with Peter Straub," *American Fantasy*, February 1982, pp. 8-26.
2. Gagne, p. 10.
3. Gregory, p. 14.
4. Gagne, p. 10.
5. Gregory, p. 14.
6. Gagne, p. 11.
7. Ibid.
8. Gagne, p. 13.
9. Ibid.
10. Gagne, p. 13.
11. Gagne, p.15.
12. Stephen King, *Danse Macabre* (New York: Berkley Books, 1982), p. 244; Jennifer Dunning, "Behind the Best Sellers: Peter Straub," *New York Times Book Review.* May 20, 1979, p. 56; and Gagne, p. 14.
13. Gregory, p. 13.
14. King, p. 250; see also Gagne, p. 15.
15. Gregory, p. 14.
16. King, pp. 249-250.
17. Gregory, p. 20.
18. King, pp. 249-50.
19. Gagne, p. 15.
20. Gagne, p. 16.
21. Gagne, p. 26.
22. Gregory, p. 15.
23. Gregory, p. 19.
24. Gagne, p. 18.
25. Peter Straub, "The 'General,' the *Dragon,* Carlos Fuentes, P. S.: The Story's Story," *The General's Wife* (West Kingston, RI: Donald M. Grant, Publisher, Inc., 1982), p. 21.
26. Gregory, p. 15.
27. Straub, p. 25.
28. Straub, p. 15.
29. Straub, p. 23.

BIBLIOGRAPHY

Dunning, Jennifer. "Behind the Best Sellers: Peter Straub." *New York Times Book Review*, May 20, 1979, p.56.

Gagne, Paul. "An Interview with Peter Straub." *American Fantasy*, February 1982, pp.8-26.

Gregory, Jay. "TZ Interview: Peter Straub." *Twilight Zone Magazine*, May 1981, pp.13-16.

King, Stephen. *Danse Macabre*. New York, Berkley Books, 1982.

_____. *'Salem's Lot*. New York, Signet Books, 1976.

Straub, Peter. "The General, The *Dragon*, Carlos Fuentes, P.S.: The Story's Story." *The General's Wife*. West Kingston, RI: Donald M. Grant, Publisher, Inc., 1982.

_____. *Ghost Story*. New York: Pocket Books, 1979.

_____. *If You Could See Me Now*. New York: Pocket Books, 1979.

_____. *Julia*. New York: Pocket Books, 1979.

_____. *Shadowland*. New York: Berkley Books, 1981.

POETRY OF DARKNESS:
THE HORROR FICTION OF
FRITZ LEIBER
by Michael E. Stamm

Eldritch words like these are flying,
Voices through the high air crying.
You whose sleep was too uneasy,
You may hear them, rising, dying.
—"Demons of the Upper Air, IIX" (1969)

If any writer can be considered the Grand Master of fantasy among living writers, that writer would have to be Fritz Leiber. In a career spanning the past half-century, Leiber has won (at last count) nine Hugo awards, four Nebulas (from the Science Fiction Writers of America), four World Fantasy awards, and two British Fantasy awards, as well as several less-well-known prizes. More than awards, of course, are his achievements themselves, the stories. It is difficult to find an anthology of science fiction or fantasy or horror stories that *lacks* a Leiber entry: stories like "The Ship Sails at Midnight" or "A Pail of Air" or "Bazaar of the Bizarre," to name three of hundreds. For a man whose name is—quite incomprehensibly—almost unknown outside the field of fantasy and science fiction, though almost (if not really) revered within it, Fritz Leiber has written some of the most important and innovative science fiction, fantasy and horror fiction ever produced. It would take a good-sized book to do justice to his horror stories alone; this article can serve only as an introduction to them.

Fritz [Reuter] Leiber [Jr.] was born in Chicago on Christmas Eve, 1910, to the noted Shakespearean actors Fritz and Virginia Bronson Leiber. There may have been an element of magic, or sorcery, in being born on such a day, to such parents; in any case, it has a great deal to do with Leiber's love of Shakespeare and the theatre, and the fact that he has perhaps the finest ear for language of any writer of fantasy or science fiction, and is in that respect rivaled by few writers of any kind. Leiber spent his youth with relatives, mostly in the Chicago area, and with his parents when they weren't on tour; he joined them on the stage in his father's company (as "Francis Lathrop") in its last seasons, 1934-35, after earning a Ph.B. in the biological sciences. In 1936 he married the English poet and writer Jonquil Stephens; their marriage lasted until her death in 1969, and they had one son, Justin, who is a professor of philosophy and author of the science fiction novel *Beyond Rejection* (1980). Along the way Leiber flirted briefly with a career as an Episcopalian minister, taught speech and drama for a year, was for four years a writer/editor for an encyclopedia publisher, spent part of World War II as an inspector for Douglas Aircraft, served as an associate editor of *Science Digest* for twelve years, and taught at the annual summer Clarion Science Fiction Writers' Workshop for its first few years. For the rest, he wrote; and he still writes.

> There's still a black, shivery outside,
> you know—a weird realm from which men
> shrink in terror. Science hasn't done away
> with it. Nothing will ever do away with it.
>
> —FL, 1946

In November of 1936—aided by his wife Jonquil, who broke the epistolary ice—Fritz Leiber began corresponding with H.P. Lovecraft, creator of the now famous "Cthulhu Mythos" and author of such classics tales as "The Rats in the Walls" and "The Colour Out of Space." Lovecraft was ill and lived only another four-and-a-half months, but the correspondence between him and Leiber was extensive while it lasted. His influence on Leiber was almost as great as Shakespeare's if not as great, though its form was seldom as obvious (and then only much later, in deliberate tribute) as it was in the cases of other Lovecraft correspondents like Robert Bloch or Robert E. Howard.

Leiber's first effort at imaginative fiction was begun in 1934 as was the tale that eventually became "Adept's Gambit," the first story written (though not the first published) in the continuing saga of his sword-and-sorcery heroes, Fafhrd and the Gray Mouser, characters created by Leiber's lifelong friend Harry Otto Fischer. An uneasy mixture of fantasy and history adventure, the story in its early forms did not sell; Leiber's first professional sale was not made until the publication of "Two Sought Adventure" (now known as "The Jewels in the Forest"), another Fafhrd-Mouser tale, in 1939.

In the realm of horror fiction, something subtle but important happened with the publication of "The Automatic Pistol" in 1940. Leiber's first horror story, it also marked the first appearance of a theme that recurs in much of his fiction since then. "The Automatic Pistol" is the tale of a handgun, and of the gangster who owns it and treats it like a pet—or a loved one. It is, in fact, no ordinary weapon, but something that might be the 20th-century equivalent of a witch's familiar; and by itself the gun murders the man who killed its owner. It's an aspect of that "black, shivery outside," that "weird realm" whose denizens may change their shapes to fit their times—but the darkness inside never changes.

The 1940s were a productive period for Fritz Leiber. 1941 saw the appearance of—among others—the nightmarish "The Power of the Puppets," a macabre tale of physical horror and puppetry almost as grim as M.R. James' (by whose work Leiber was also influenced) "The Story of a Disappearance and an Appearance." "Smoke Ghost" was also published in 1941, and its tale of malign powers taking shape in the smoke and soot of a modern American city is another of Leiber's abiding interests: the concept that modern megalopoli take on or create certain non-human powers or forces. "It would grow out of the real world. It would reflect the tangled, sordid, vicious things...And it would be very grimy...It wouldn't moan. But it would mutter unintelligibly, and twitch at your sleeve." The idea is the stuff of nightmares, as the spectre of an all-too-tangible, M.R. Jamesian horror with no connection with or sympathy for humanity.

"The Hound" was published in 1942, and continued in the tradition of "Smoke Ghost" with its tale of a savage, monstrous shadow-thing stalking the protagonist from the hive-busy heart of the city out through the desolation of new suburbs; the title is perhaps an acknowledgment that the story is Leiber's approach to ideas used in H.P. Lovecraft's grisly story of the same title. "The Hound" was followed by "Spider Mansion," in itself a minor tale of the dreadful results of a man's meddling with growth hormones; the pulpiest of pulp stories, it does not seem a Leiber tale at all unless one learns by chance the story of its writing. At the time Leiber was having trouble finding a metier that would guarantee consistent sales to *Weird Tales*, then the best and certainly the most famous market for horror fiction. In talking to an Old Hand who'd been selling to *WT* for years, Leiber got a list of the sort of things the magazine could be expected to like in weird fiction: giant spiders, mad doctors, lonely haunted houses, giant dwarfs, innocent bystanders, etc. As an experiment—with definite humorous overtones—Fritz Leiber put *all* of these disparate elements into one story—"Spider Mansion"—and submitted it to *Weird Tales*—which bought it immediately...

1942 also saw the appearance of "The Hill and the Hole," a little-known but strange and horrifying tale of a hole that looks like a hill, and of the bony, undead things that guard its never-explained secrets with a grim and dusty death.

Fritz Leiber's first novel, *Conjure Wife*, was published in *Unknown Worlds* magazine in April 1943. Though it did not achieve book publication for another decade, the novel is a classic of horror fiction. It is the story of anthropologist Norman Saylor, who is what he appears to be, and of his wife Tansy, who is considerably more than that. The premise of the novel is that all women are witches, carrying on the ancient traditions and protecting and helping their men

20

through sorcery, never speaking of it even to each other except perhaps as mother-to-daughter. The tension of the story begins when Norman Saylor discovers—though of course he does not *believe*—that his wife is a witch, and forces her to stop what he considers to be her ineffectual rituals. She *is* a witch, of course, and dreadful things start to happen when she can no longer protect herself or her husband from the sorceries of other faculty wives who are witches, as she is, but far less scrupulous about their motives and self-serving goals. Stated this badly, the premise is unlikely, to say the least, but Leiber's careful blending of reality—Hempnell College, where the story takes place, is modeled loosely but with considerable insight on Occidental College in Los Angeles, where he taught speech and drama—with the mechanics of sorcery is impeccable, and the story is absolutely convincing. At one point a cement gargoyle is given ghastly life, to seek out the couple and destroy them, and Leiber's deliberately workmanlike prose shifts into poetry as Tansy frantically works her magic against the thing: "But on [Norman's] retina was burned the incandescent track of the lightning, whose multiple streams, racing toward the upreared stony form, had converged upon it as if drawn together by a sevenfold knot." The climax of horror comes at the end of Chapter 14, in a shocking scene that has few equals anywhere in horror literature, as Norman, racing to save his wife from the concentrated powers of her enemies, finds that he was one minute too late...

The novel—fortunately!—does not end there, but reaches its end in a tale of nightmarish horror and savage sorcery, wielded on the one hand by ruthless witches of long standing and on the other by Norman Saylor, who through the mechanisms of symbolic logic has reduced that magic to its simplest form—but it remains magic, though it is couched in modern terms, echoing Leiber's theme of old powers in new guises. *Conjure Wife* is one of the most memorable novels in a field that has produced no small number of classic tales.

1947 saw the publication—by Arkham House, perhaps the greatest name in publishers of horror and dark fantasy—of Fritz Leiber's first collection, *Night's Black Agents*. (The title comes from *Macbeth*, III, ii—Shakespeare again.) Besides "The Automatic Pistol," "Smoke Ghost," "The Hill and the Hole," and "The Hound," as well as two Fafhrd-Gray Mouser stories and the eerily poignant "The Man Who Never Grew Young," the book contains "The Inheritance," a grittily detailed, rather mundane story of a murderer and his posthumous exposure—by his nephew—through dreams and more than dreams; "Diary in the Snow," a very Lovecraftian tale of alien invasion; and "The Dreams of Albert Moreland." Leiber's love of chess—at which he once held an Expert rating, and which will reappear in later stories—makes its first appearance in his horror fiction here. The story, of a master chess-player and the games he played in his sleep—and beyond sleep—on whose outcome the fate of the world depended—is a Lovecraftian tale that outdoes Lovecraft in its use of symbolism, atmosphere, and its skill in dialogue, with which Lovecraft had no ability.

In 1951 Marshall McLuhan published a book called *The Mechanical Bride*, in which he referred at length to Fritz Leiber's story "The Girl with the Hungry Eyes" as a work of considerable importance with its perception of the uses of sex, and its sublimation into something more than sex, in the world of advertising. The story was published in 1949 and was considerably ahead of its time. It is a story of eroticism of sorts—a longtime fascination with Leiber, and something he has been honest enough to admit not being entirely comfortable with—and of emotional vampirism, something considerably more horrible than the simple bloodlust of earlier succubae.

"In the X-Ray" was also published in 1949; its secret, the rare and gruesome but very real biological error of one of a pair of would-be twins absorbing the other long prior to birth, only to have the other, or part of it, start to grow in the survivor's body suddenly, unexplainably, long *after* birth, harks back to "The Power of the Puppets" and adds in grimness what the story lacks in complexity.

During the 1950s Fritz Leiber turned to science fiction, for the most part, though 1950 saw the publication of "The Dead Man," a minor but often-reprinted story of an experiment in hypnosis gone awry in a manner more or less the reverse of Poe's "Facts in the Case of M. Valdemar." Leiber's science fiction contained its eerie elements: "A Pail of Air"'s picture of a world torn from its sun, layered in many feet of ice and covered in an oxygen 'snow'; and Leiber's second novel, *Gather, Darkness!* (serialized in 1943, published as a book in 1950), which, with its future world of priests and scientist-witches, has a peculiar horror all its own. *Conjure Wife* was issued as a book in 1953.

After a long dry spell in the field, Leiber published "A Deskful of Girls" in 1958. The story is one of a science—psychoanalysis, a science of sorts—at the service of sorcery, and an unscrupulous practitioner who strips his female patients of certain aspects of self, each aspect a ghostgirl, an exquisitely erotic, semi-tangible prisoner. The climax comes when one such patient, an actress ruthless and self-serving by inclination, and all too aware of what has happened to her, takes charge of her other selves and turns them on their jailer. The story is another sample of Leiber's interest in the erotic as well as a further example of his absolutely unique view of things. This uniqueness was reinforced by "Schizo Jimmie," a relatively unknown story which appeared 1959, about a man who was quite literally a carrier of insanity, as Typhoid Mary carried typhus and as untouched by it—and who *knew* it, and used it for his own ends.

"Mariana" was published in 1960. At midnight on Halloween, 1981, at the World Fantasy Convention in Berkeley, Fritz Leiber sat on the edge of an empty stage before a darkened ballroom and read the story aloud in his deep actor's voice, and a roomful of people sat absolutely spellbound. The story, of a young wife who finds with the push of each button on a hidden panel that nothing in her far-future world is real—including her, is nominally science fiction, is closer to fantasy, and yet has a quality of darkness and mystery shared by the best horror fiction. "A Bit of the Dark World" appeared in 1962; its story of alien forces surrounding and finally overwhelming a lonely California mountain house is again Lovecraftian in inspiration but outdoes the master in its use of dialogue and characterization; the people are more real and one cares more what happens to them.

"The Black Gondolier" appeared in an original Arkham House anthology in 1964. Like the science-fictional "The Man Who Made Friends with Electricity" of two years before, but perhaps more horrifying because of the subterranean, ancient and organic nature of its subject, it concerns the baleful powers and influence of a planetwide substance or phenomenon—in this case, crude oil. Set in Venice, California, once a resort modeled after its Adriatic namesake and now almost a slum, pocked throughout with the nodding, thumping machinery of oil wells, the story makes full use of the blackness, the thickness, the viscosity, the dark vitality of oil. The story is a nightmare, the more so since what seems to the protagonist as wild paranoia turns out to be simply justifiable terror.

Shadows with Eyes, Fritz Leiber's second collection of horror stories, was published in 1964, containing "A Bit of the Dark World," "The Dead Man," "The Power of the Puppets," "Schizo Jimmie," "The Man Who Made Friends with Electricity," and "A Deskful of Girls." 1964 also saw the appearance of "Midnight in the Mirror World," a deceptively simple tale of a man who sees his fate—in the guise of a mysterious woman, long dead—approaching him in the compound reflections of mirrors.

"To Arkham and the Stars" was written for *The Dark Brotherhood*, a volume of tributes to H.P. Lovecraft which appeared in 1966. It is a loving tale of a man's journey to Lovecraft's (fictional) Arkham and his meetings with characters out of Lovecraft's fiction, characters who have survived the threats of ancient, alien evils and live on to fight again. It was followed by the award-winning "Gonna Roll the Bones," which was published in Harlan Ellison's landmark anthology *Dangerous Visions* in 1967. The story is an eerie, phantasmagorical adventure, almost an allegory or perhaps the stuff of legend, of a man who ventures from his home on a gutted Earth to gamble with Death for fame, fortune, and his life—or so he thinks. "Gonna

Roll the Bones" is notable for its delightful inventiveness, its eerily real yet fantastic atmosphere, and its deep warm humanity.

In the late '60s and early '70s Fritz Leiber expanded and reorganized much of his Fafhrd-Gray Mouser series, and took on the duties of book reviewer/critic for *Fantastic* magazine for several years, demonstrating in no uncertain terms his ability as essayist and critic as well as fictioneer. .

1974 saw the publication of "Midnight by the Morphy Watch," a chess horror story of an older man—Stirf Ritter-Rebil, a quasi-anagrammatic twist of his full name, Fritz Reuter Leiber—who finds the half-mythical presentation watch of 19th-century chess genius Paul Morphy and traces it from its original owner through the hands of the greatest chess masters—men who all went mad, or died, or vanished—and of what Ritter-Rebil does to rid himself of the watch before it can destroy him. "Midnight by the Morphy Watch" is the first of a kind of series of stories whose unifying elements are that they are all set in places that Leiber knows well and/or places in which he lives or has lived, and whose protagonists are modeled to one degree or another on Fritz Leiber himself.

"The Glove," second in this quasi-series, was published in 1975. It is the story of a particularly unpleasant crime and the betrayal of the criminal by a glove he had worn in its commission. It is very like the Victorian "this really happened" ghost story in that the protagonist is only tangentially connected with the events of the tale, and the mechanisms of the supernatural are pat but still unexplained. "Belsen Express" (1975) is as close to a purely psychological horror story as Leiber ever gets; it is the story of a man with a fascination with, and a paranoid fear of, the horrors of the Nazi death camps, though World War II is long over, and of what happens to him—or what his mind does to him.

"The Terror from the Depths" (1976) is another overt tribute to H.P. Lovecraft, being the tale of a young man whose life falls afoul of the influences of the Elder Gods of Lovecraft's Cthulhu Mythos. The story is very carefully constructed in Lovecraftian fashion, set in California but with the introduction of (or references to) known characters from Lovecraft's own fiction. The protagonist's name is Georg Reuter Fischer, another Leiber in-joke, drawn from Georg (Mann, a longtime friend in Chicago), (Fritz) Reuter (Leiber), and (Harry Otto) Fischer (Leiber's lifelong friend and correspondent); the character also has a congenital twisted foot, a characteristic of the youth of Fritz Leiber's father. Considering the care and attention with which this quasi-Lovecraft tale is constructed, it ends on a sharply grim note, with the young protagonist dead in a particularly gruesome manner at the hands—or whatever—of some avatar of the Elder Gods.

"Dark Wings" (1976) is in some ways Leiber's most disturbing tale of horror, fraught with symbolism both overt and covert. It is the story of two young women who find themselves almost soulmates from the word go, speculating on shared likes, dislikes, physical peculiarities, and the possibility that they are, unbeknownst to each other, twins, separated at birth and only finding each other by accident; their sisterly intimacy progresses to a slowly shared physical intimacy moving from simple closeness to the erotic and suddenly over a shocking edge into rape, for one of them is not female at all, or perhaps not even human. The story ends with the crescendoing repetition of a simple word—"there, there, there, *there*," a repetition which assumes in the reader's mind the pounding sexual impact of a hammer.

Fritz Leiber's second novel of the supernatural, *Our Lady of Darkness* (the title drawn from a chapter of Thomas De Quincey's *Suspiria De Profundis* [1856]—"And *her* name is *Mater Tenebrarum*—Our Lady of Darkness") was published in 1978; it was serialized in 1977 as "The Pale Brown Thing." It is in the same line as "Midnight by the Morphy Watch"—protagonist Franz Western bears considerable resemblance to Fritz Leiber and even inhabits Leiber's apartment in his apartment-building on Geary Street in San Francisco. In a sense the story is the culmination of many of Leiber's recurrent themes. The overall mood is the horror of cities: specifically, that once a city reaches a certain size, it take on its own horrid, unhuman kind of consciousness. (At the same time there is a trace of tongue-in-cheek here, in that the San Francisco of *Our Lady of Darkness*, though long a locus of weird forces, did not achieve this weird quasi-sentience until the Transamerica pyramid was completed.) There is also an undercurrent of the erotic, both in Western's relationship with the much younger woman who will ultimately be his savior, and in the conception of the anthropomorphic scatter of books-on-bedside which Western refers to as his Scholar's Mistress. And of course Our Lady Of Darkness herself, the horrid construct of lifeless matter, of which there has been nothing as unnerving since the ghost-thing with its twisted face of crumpled linen in M. R. James' "'Oh Whistle, and I'll Come to You, My Lad'," contains a certain erotic element—straight from a nightmare.

For those well-read in horror fiction, as well as in other genres, the novel is a delight beyond being a classic tale of horror. The story is a congeries of in-jokes and name-dropping; Dashiell Hammett, San Francisco habitue and creator of Sam Spade, is a minor character, as is weird-fantasist Clark Ashton Smith; in the name of "megalopolisomancist" Thibaut de Castries there is an at times overt reference to H.P. Lovecraft's long-standing self-conferred nickname of (Grandpa) Theobald. There is a minor character who adopts the name Fah Lo Suee, the name of the delightfully deadly daughter of Fu Manchu. And that is just the start of it. *Our Lady of Darkness* is perhaps a shade (!) less good than *Conjure Wife*—but that leaves it plenty of room to be very good indeed.

"Black Glass" (1978) is not precisely a horror story; but this tale of an older man in New York, who in reaching the top of the World Trade Center either has a hallucinatory experience or actually passes through time into an unimaginable future where the city has been inundated in hundreds of feet of something that is not dust or cobwebs or soot but partakes of all three, has elements of horror in it. There is a kind of dreamy, phantasmal quality about the story; one could wish that it were the first part of a longer tale, as perhaps it may turn out to be.

1979's "The Button Molder" (the title is drawn from a strange character in Ibsen's *Peer Gynt*) is like "Black Glass" and *Our Lady of Darkness* and others; its main character might be Fritz Leiber himself, though of course it is not—not really. The story is eerie and impressive but difficult to define or describe; like "The Glove," its important aspects are not really the supernatural elements but the evocation of the reality in which they appear, or seem to appear, that makes them work so well. The tale has the dark inevitability of a dream, where the end is sensed long before it is actually seen or experienced.

April 1984 saw the publication of a major Leiber collection, *The Ghost Light*. It contains, among numerous others, the poignant "Four Ghosts in Hamlet" (1965), which is not really a ghost story but a story of people and love and understanding. Also included are "Midnight by the Morphy Watch," "Black Glass," and "Gonna Roll the Bones," as well as the title story, a tale of memories and lies and the final vengeance of the past, in which the supernatural elements, impressive as they are, are equalled by Leiber's mastery of characterization and sheer storytelling to create a truly memorable story.

The Ghost Light is also of great value for Leiber fans in that almost a third of its length is devoted to "Not So Much Disorder and Not So Early Sex," a fascinatingly discursive autobiographical essay on life, sex, love, writing, and more.

There are other stories, good stories, for which there is now no room here; I have tried to cover the high spots, the most notable works, with additions chosen strictly at my own whim. And there is, of course, the consideration that Fritz Leiber's work seldom fits neatly into any genre or category; a particular story can be considered to be as representative of fantasy or science fiction as it can be of horror, in some cases. That is the main reason why I have not dealt with any of Leiber's sword-and-sorcery (let credit fall where it is due: Fritz Leiber coined that particular term), though Fafhrd-and-Mouser stories like "The Howling Tower" or "The Sunken Land" or "The Bleak Shore" have much to recommend them from the standpoint of horror, as well.

Some of his science fiction can be considered the same way; the very title "The Mind Spider," for instance, is enough to make some cringe.

The ghost light is an old theatrical tradition; one light is always left burning, somewhere backstage, so that ghosts will stay away. It took someone like Fritz Leiber to wonder, "What if you had a light to which ghosts would come?" instead. There is a dark poignancy in the thought, and a weird kind of warmth.

Fifteen years ago, in an appreciation of Fritz Leiber written for a special Leiber edition of *The Magazine of Fantasy and Science Fiction*, Judith Merril wrote that if it was his empathy which made Leiber, then almost 60, able to communicate so clearly with people a fraction his age. To that empathy I would add honesty, and a real sense of the ludicrous as well as the mysterious; perhaps they all add up to one thing for which there isn't a name yet. Fritz Leiber writes as well as—though very differently than—he ever did before, after fifty years at his trade; I am one of many who hope he will continue to do so for many years to come.

[I would like to thank Joseph Dean Belcher for his invaluable bibliographical and critical help in the research for this essay—MES]

SUGGESTED BIBLIOGRAPHY

The following is a brief list of Fritz Leiber's horror fiction currently in print—a woefully small amount—as well as some titles which might be available secondhand or through specialty dealers without inordinate trouble or expense. With luck, some time soon an enterprising publisher will see fit to issue at least one volume, and perhaps more, of Fritz Leiber's incomparable dark fantasies.

In print (as of July 1984):

The Ghost Light, Berkley Books, 1984, $7.95 (trade paper)
Our Lady of Darkness, Ace Books, 1984, $2.50 (paper)
Conjure Wife, Ace Books, 1981, $2.50 (paper)
Night's Black Agents, Sphere [Great Britain], 1977 (paper)
Heroes and Horrors, ed. Stuart Davis Schiff, Whispers Press, 1978, $12.00 (hardcover)

Available secondhand (with luck):

Night's Black Agents, Arkham House, 1947 (hardcover); Berkley, 1978 (paper, adds two stories); Gregg Press, 1980 (hardcover, reprint of the Berkley edition).

Night Monsters, Panther [Great Britain], 1974 [contains twice as many stories as the American collection (Ace, 1969, with *The Green Millennium*) of the same name] (paper)

Heroes and Horrors, ed. Stuart Schiff, Pocket Books, 1978 (paper)

The Book of Fritz Leiber, DAW Books, 1975 (paper)

Shadows with Eyes, Ballantine Books, 1964 (paper) (quite rare)

Finding any of these will be well worth the effort. Good Hunting!

TALES OF CHILDHOOD AND THE GRAVE:
RAY BRADBURY'S HORROR FICTION
by Darrell Schweitzer

Ray Bradbury's horror fiction belongs primarily to the first phase of his career, when he was in his twenties and just beginning to find his voice as a writer. Later, the Weird Muse deserted him, and attempts to return to the former mode were unsuccessful. But the young Bradbury made major contributions to the supernatural story. His first collection of such work, *Dark Carnival*, (1947) has been called "the *Dubliners* of American fantasy" by Stephen King. His influence is clearly visible in the work of Richard Matheson, Charles Beaumont, Dennis Etchison, and Charles L. Grant. Numerous others have acknowledged their debt to him.

His horror fiction is in some ways difficult to evaluate. It is so much about childhood, and formed from the perceptions and memories of children that the age of the *reader* becomes a key factor. It is best to begin Bradbury early, somewhere between the ages of twelve and fifteen. He has a strong impact on teenaged readers, who can not only recognize the characters and situations from their own recent memory, but easily identify with the emotions the stories evoke. At sixteen it is far easier to remember what it was like to be twelve than at forty. Bradbury is often thoroughly authentic at that level. But at the same time, many of his early horror stories seem *plotted* by a child—for all they are the work of an adult, superbly literate author. They contain logic lapses and gross superficialities which a child might not notice, but which can ruin the story for an adult.

Reactions can be extremely subjective. For the record, I read most of the Bradbury horror stories at the proper age, in my teens. Coming back to them now, at thirty-three, they are not all as I remembered them. "The Next in Line," which once seemed diffuse and boring, has gained considerable power. "Jack-in-the-Box," a wonderful old favorite, now looks contrived and silly, for all I can see its central image retains its appeal. Happily, "Homecoming," "Uncle Einar," "The Emissary," and many of the others are *still* wonderful.

Certainly, at the very beginning, Bradbury was not especially promising. We first see him, in his own reminiscences, and in those of others, as a perhaps overly intrusive youth who hung around Los Angeles fandom in the late '30s, always entirely too eager to shove his latest masterpiece under the noses of available professionals. The stories were typical amateur work. A few of them have survived, reprinted from fanzines in various Sam Moskowitz anthologies.

Nevertheless, Leigh Brackett, Edmond Hamilton, and Henry Kuttner took the time to coach him, and their efforts paid off. Eventually.

"Pendulum," his first professionally published story, is intensely unimpressive, a rewrite of a fanzine story, from his own publication, *Futuria Fantasia.*[1] The professional version gives the impression of being an extremely marginal item which barely managed to squeak by in a fringe market (*Super Science Stories*, November 1941) with the collaborative help of Henry Hasse. Hasse was not a major name himself, but he was an established professional, the author of one highly regarded story, "He Who Shrank," and his presence may have made the difference.

It would be years before Bradbury attracted any notice for science-fiction. The focus of the period was on John W. Campbell's *Astounding Science Fiction* (today called *Analog*), and Bradbury's two appearances there (both in the September 1943 issue) were among the weakest fiction that magazine ever published. His contemporaries were developing faster. Heinlein, de Camp, Hubbard, Asimov, Eric Frank Russell, and other "Golden Age" writers held center stage, and nobody noticed the author of such routine filler as "Morgue Ship" and "The Piper" in *Planet Stories* and *Thrilling Wonder Stories*.

But in *Weird Tales*, Bradbury struck out on his own. *Weird Tales* had been the foremost (usually the only) fantasy, as opposed to science-fiction, pulp magazine since 1923. It was a little past its prime; its great editor, Farnsworth Wright, and many of the contributors of the magazine's own "Golden Age," Robert E. Howard, H.P. Lovecraft, Henry Whitehead, etc., were dead. Others, like Clark Ashton Smith, had virtually ceased writing. Further, another John W. Campbell magazine, *Unknown*, was providing serious competition, not merely with higher word rates, but a whole new style of fantasy. But *Weird Tales* was not yet seriously into its decline. The climate was right for a talented new writer to arrive. When Bradbury did, the new editor, Dorothy McIllwraith, soon realized she had made a major find.

Bradbury's first sale to *Weird Tales*, however, was still apprentice work. "The Candle," (November 1942) is a trite story of a supernatural murder that twists back on its perpetrator (in editorialese, "the biter bitten," still a stock device of horror comics). Henry Kuttner wrote the final 200 words, or at least revised them to the point the story is almost a collaboration.

Then something happened. It may have been a matter of influences. Bradbury has mentioned spending a summer reading Thomas Wolfe, Ernest Hemingway, and other mainstream writers, to get an idea of what good *writing* was about, then applying what he had learned to the pulps. Certainly, as often happens with developing young writers, something suddehly clicked, and his second *Weird Tales* story was an enormous improvement over the first.

"The Wind" (March 1943) is a subtle horror story, about a man slowly absorbed into the wind, told in a stark, spare prose comparable to that of the best "literary" writers of the period.

In the May 1943 issue, he showed he could do it again, with "The Crowd." Again, the writing was far above the pulp average, and the concept behind the story was both novel and strikingly contemporary. Not content to write about clanking specters in Gothic castles, Bradbury found his horrors in modern, everyday life. There is no more modern sort of death than a traffic accident. The story is about one man's discovery that the crowd always forms around such accidents is made up of the *same* people, ghosts of previous victims, existing in a kind of limbo.

"The Scythe" (July 1943) also demonstrates the "new" Bradbury style and the rapidly flowering Bradbury imagination. Again, in stark, clear prose, we explore the peculiarities of death, as a farmer displaced by the Depression finds himself handling *the* scythe, which causes people to die as he reaps wheat.

These stories are far in advance of any science fiction Bradbury was writing in this period.

By the November 1943 issue, he was a popular enough contributor that the editor had him write an autobiographical sketch for the magazine. In it, he described his childhood fascination with the uncanny, and, more significantly, early childhood fears of a monster waiting at the top of the stairs. Then he remarked:

> I don't particularly care about ghosts, vampires, or werewolves; they've been killed with repetition....There are good stories in everyday things. Trains, crowds, motor-cars, submarines, dogs—the wind around the house. I'd like to use them more. And there's much good stuff buried in the green leaves of childhood and the heaped dead leaves of old age.[2] I want to get at that, too. I want to write about humans; and add an unusual, unexpected twist.

Thus, at the age of twenty-three, Bradbury had had the essential insight which was to shape the rest of his career. He turned inward, to his own memories and feelings; and to his own observations of the people around him. His science fiction was still contrived and imitative, but in weird fantasy, he was already beginning to lead. True, other writers, notably Fritz Leiber (with "The Hound," "Smoke Ghost," and *Conjure Wife*), were working in the same vein at the same time, and William Sloane had written two very modernistic horror novels in the late '30s, *To Walk the Night* and *The Edge of Running Water*, but Bradbury had defined the direction in which horror fiction was to go, away from haunted English country houses, dark forests, and either traditional or Lovecraftian monsters, toward big cities and their suburbs, and into the mind. There is a direct line of development from these early Bradbury stories to the works of Stephen King, Peter Straub, and all the rest.

His story in that November 1943 issue was, ironically, a misstep, "The Ducker," about Johnny Choir, a soldier who thinks he is still ten years old. Thus, war is a children's game, and he can duck bullets. He denies death, and can't be killed. While the prose is good, the story can only be described as dumb. It rings false. A real soldier like that would have been run out of the army as a mental case. He seems uncomfortably close to being, not some kind of crazy idealist, but retarded. (One misstep followed another too. There was a sequel, "Bang! You're Dead!" in the September 1944 issue.)

Nevertheless, the story makes use of the two basic Bradbury themes from this period: childhood and death. A remarkable number of his mid-1940s stories are about death: macabre gimmicks, fears, coming to terms with death, or, as with "The Ducker," some sort of denial. He had looked into his own psyche and found intimations of mortality, but at the same time the child in him tried to say it wasn't true.

"Reunion" (March 1944) combines both themes: an orphaned child, neglected by adults, retreats into an attic filled with the memorabilia of his dead parents. Before he is interrupted, he almost manages to bring them back, by wishing, but at the same time he is close to death himself from thirst and starvation.

"The Lake" (May 1944) is about coming to terms with a childhood death. When a twelve-year-old boy's eleven-year-old sweetheart drowns, he doesn't understand, and calls out to her from the shore. Later, as a married adult, aged twenty-two, he is present as the girl's body is finally found. The hero may not be as emotionally backward as Johnny Choir, but he still has never accepted the reality of death, and now reaches a frightening level of understanding. The dead girl's ghost has kept a tryst with the protagonist, building half a sandcastle by the water's edge, so he can build the other half, as they had always done before; but this seems less a terrible revelation than the fact that she is *still* eleven.

In "There Was an Old Woman" (July 1944) the title character does Johnny Choir one better. To her, the idea of dying is ridiculous. This is her "new philosophy." By sheer, cantankerous will, she is about to go to the morgue, reclaim her own body, and continue living.

Sometimes, though, the denial of death has less pleasant consequences. In "The Emissary," a small boy is bedridden, and visited every day by a favorite teacher. She, and his faithful dog, are his only contacts with the outside world. Then the teacher is killed, but the dog brings her back. The ending is not sentimental, but understatedly horrific. It is presumably the teacher's rotted corpse, dug up by the dog, which shambles up the boy's bedroom door at the end. The boy no more understands death than does the soldier of "The Ducker," but he is in for a hideous lesson.

"The Emissary" was not sold to *Weird Tales*, but to the more prestigious *Unknown Worlds*, the companion magazine to *Astounding*. It would have been a major step up for its author had the story actually appeared, but, unfortunately *Unknown* succumbed to World War II paper shortages, and the story did not see print until *Dark Carnival* in 1947.

Bradbury wrote steadily for *Weird Tales* throughout the middle 1940s. He had a story in every issue except one between March 1943 and September 1945. But at the same time, he was expanding his range, and his markets, as the abortive sale to *Unknown* showed.

He turned to detective fiction, and by 1944 was a regular in such publications as *Dime Mystery Magazine* and *Detective Tales*. These pulps did not feature so much classical whodunits as terror tales. They were the toned-down descendants of the quasi-pornographic "weird menace" magazines which had been a fad in the late '30s, chock-full of sex and sadism and titles like "Hell Brides of Satan's Lust." Bradbury's detective fiction is outrageously grotesque, hardboiled almost to the point of burlesque. It is very closely related to the work he was doing in *Weird Tales* at the same time. Indeed, some of the stories in *Weird Tales* may have been detective magazine rejects, and vice-versa.

The best of the detective/crime efforts were collected in *A Memory of Murder* (1984). In the introduction he describes the way he wrote in the early days:

> ...every Monday I wrote a first draft of any story that leaped into my head. On Tuesday I wrote a second draft. On Wednesday, Thursday, and Friday, third, fourth, and fifth versions followed. On Saturday the final draft went into the mail. On Sunday I collapsed on the beach with Leigh [Brackett], and on Monday I was back starting a new story.

Indeed, the detective stories show considerable signs of haste and shallow conception, as Bradbury wrote anything that came to him, whether with conviction or not. Such stories are never as convincing or as moving as his very best efforts, because the emotions in them are more contrived than genuine, but they do have a certain macabre zest. The most famous of them, "The Small Assassin," also has the benefit of a striking gimmick: a fiendishly clever baby which murders both its parents.

He played endless permutations with the basic paraphernalia of the murder tale, switching viewpoints, until he had a story told by the corpse ("It Burns Me Up"), or another in which one Siamese twin is murdered, so the other must solve the crime ("Corpse Carnival"). There is even, shades of "The Ducker," a set of stories about a midget ex-detective who harasses criminals to death. He is *so* clever that they never shoot him. He always turns them against each other first. This is not really believable, but Bradbury uses a standard pulp-writer's technique: appealing razzle-dazzle which dampens the reader's critical faculties. Doc Savage, Tarzan, Jules de Grandin, The Shadow, and all the rest aren't really believable either, if you stop and think about them. The point is that you aren't supposed to. But again, this does not make for serious, emotionally intense fiction, either. The reader is entertained, though seldom moved.

And, there are novel (or excessively gory) methods of murder. In "A Careful Man Dies," the victim/protagonist is a hemophiliac, who is lured onto the beach by a woman, who scratches his sunburned back, so he won't know he is bleeding to death until it is too late. (Never content to be conventional, Bradbury narrates this story in the second person present.) In "Hell's Half Hour," a blind man is mysteriously, brutally beaten to death over the course of a half an hour. Why did it take so long? Because the killer, too, was blind. The killers in "The Long Night" do their work by holding the victim's head into a furnace.

The detective stories are, as a whole, not very good. The characters in them are stereotypes, the women wanton and treacherous, the detectives tough, the criminals vicious. Sometimes, there is a definite element of parody: the midget detective keeps trying to roll cigarettes the way Sam Spade does, but they always fall apart. (Here Bradbury had touched on one of the great clichés of 1940s "tough guy" detective fiction: cigarettes as a substitute for realism.) The corpse in "It Burns Me Up," betrayed by his wife who has managed to convince the detective of her innocence, remarks at the end, in suitably clipped prose, that maybe after he's cremated some of his ashes will get in their "damned eyes." Hence the title. Is Bradbury kidding?

The stories about Mexicans tend to be the best. They have traces of sincerity the other crime stories lack. Sometime in the early 1940s, Bradbury visited Mexico, and was very taken with the people, and with the strangeness of some of their customs, particularly the death-festivals on the Day of the Dead. The matter of Mexico continues throughout the rest of his career, but first appeared in "The Long Night" in 1944 (murder and race riots in a California barrio, with Nazi instigators), and again in "The Candy Skull" (1948), in which an American tourist finds a friend's body in the catacombs where Mexicans display the corpses of people whose relatives couldn't pay the rent for graves. (As it turns out, the friend was killed by a mad bull-fighter. The protagonist barely escapes.)

The subject matter of "The Candy Skull," the Day of the Dead and Mexican catacombs, were put to much better use in "The Next in Line," which appeared as an original in *Dark Carnival*. Quite likely, Bradbury was unable to sell this story, despite its being one of his very best. It lacks even vestigial crime/detective elements, and is also not fantasy, which *Weird Tales* preferred. Further, it is quite long, and would have taken up perhaps more space than either *Weird Tales* or the detective magazines would have allowed for a story which did not really fit their category requirements.

"The Next in Line" is about an American woman who views the rotting corpses in the catacombs on the Day of the Dead and becomes obsessed with the idea that she, too, will be displayed there. By the end of the story, she is, and her husband, who lacks her sensitivity, doesn't seem to care.

In striking contrast to such wish-fulfillments as "There Was an Old Woman," this story does *not* deny death, but stares it in the face, as intensely as Poe did in "The Premature Burial" or "The Pit and the Pendulum." As a tale of unrelieved horror, it is perhaps the most powerful thing Bradbury ever wrote.

Death is seen as destruction, as sheer negation. There is nothing romantic or sentimental about it, as the woman gazes at the corpses and her husband makes banal remarks and even tries to get the cemetery keeper to sell him one as a souvenir:

> ...They stood like the naked pipes of a vast derelict calliope, their mouths cut into frantic vents. And now the great hand of mania descended on all the keys at once, and the long calliope screamed upon one hundred-throated, unending scream.
>
> Click went the camera and Joseph rolled the film. Click went the camera and Joseph rolled the film.
>
> Moreno, Morelos, Cantine, Gomez, Gutierrez, Villanousul, Ureta, Licon, Narrarro, Iturbi; Jorge, Filomena, Nena, Manuel, Jose, Tomas, Ramona. This man walked and this man sang and this man had three wives; and this man died of this, and that of that, and the third from another thing, and the fourth was shot, and the fifth was stabbed and the sixth fell straight down dead; and the seventh drank deep and died dead, and the eighth died of love...(*The October Country*, p.32)

Many of Bradbury's later stories in *Weird Tales* show the uninhibited sense of grue he had displayed in the detective magazines, and a few of them show the maturity of "The Next in Line."

"Skeleton" (September 1945) has a central gimmick as outrageous as "The Small Assassin" or "Corpse Carnival": a seeming hypochondriac becomes obsessed with the fact that there is a *skeleton*, an image of death, inside his body. It is his enemy, and the fleshman, and the bone-fiend are at war. In the end, the man is seen as a kind of jellyfish, playing on a bone flute...This is one of those stories which makes no sense at all on rational analysis, but the sheer irrationality of it has the power of a bad dream.

"The Handler" (January 1947) is a shocker by any standard, concerning a perverted undertaker, much humiliated by the people of his town, who gets revenge by arranging corpses in hideous and insulting ways, as, for example, three gossiping old biddies crammed together in a single coffin, so they can be together forever. Even more startling:

> At yet another service an old maid was the victim of a
> ghoulish arrangement. Under the silken comforter,
> parts of an old man had been buried with her. There
> she lay, insulted by cold organs, being made love to by
> hidden hands. The shock showed on her face, some-
> what. (*Bloch and Bradbury*, p.35)

In the end, the outraged corpses have *their* revenge, in an ironic manner in the best E.C. Comics tradition.[3]

"The October Game," which appeared in the 25th anniversary issue of *Weird Tales* (March 1948) is similarly gruesome, but has no fantasy element. It's about children passing around pieces of a corpse in the dark. There is a powerful, although obvious punchline. Similar fun and games occur in "Let's Play Poison," (November 1946) in which malicious children lure an adult to his death.

On a much more serious, sensitive note, "The Night" (July 1946) attempts to use the extreme immediacy of second-person present narration to capture the growing fears of a child whose older brother is out late and may be missing or dead. Here, Bradbury uses real experience, not the contrived *grand guignol* of stories like "The October Game." The child protagonist learns, for the first time, what death is, and how in the face of it, even parents are helpless. The story is not wholly successful—indeed, the second person technique seems self-conscious and forced—but it would not have been strengthened by gore and grotesquerie.

The rest of Bradbury's supernatural or horror fiction from the 1940s ranges widely in quality and tone. Sometimes he would seize on a powerful idea, but, writing in a sheer emotional outburst, fail to think his premise through. In "Interim," (*Weird Tales*, July 1947) a dead, pregnant woman gives birth in the grave. This is an awful situation, with enormous potential, but all Bradbury does is present the idea in the clumsiest possible manner: the corpses in the cemetery relate it by tapping on their coffins—in Morse Code!

"Jack-in-the-Box," another of the originals in *Dark Carnival*, has more to it, but a similar problem. A woman loses her husband to an automobile, and neurotically withdraws from this world, raising her young son in total isolation in an old house. The story is told from the boy's point of view. To him, the house is the world, and his mother and the mysterious "Teacher" are the only other living beings. This is a fascinating idea, and to a childish reader, the story presents an image of alienation as powerful as that in the early sections of Lovecraft's "The Outsider." But the adult reader wonders: has the boy never looked out a window? What about the mailman, the truant officers, etc. Has an airplane never flown overhead? The mother goes out for groceries, but this never arouses any curiosity. By the end of the story we learn that the "Teacher" is the mother in disguise, and that for ten or so years, she has never once failed in this charade. Further, the house is in an inhabited neighborhood, because when the boy gets out, he is quickly next to a traffic-filled street. Plausibility breaks down entirely. The boy, coming into the modern world, is convinced that he is dead (though he does not know what death means). This, too, is a powerful image. The story is almost a great one, but for once, a little bit of careful thinking on Bradbury's part would have helped enormously.[4]

"Black Ferris" (*Weird Tales*, May 1948) also centered on a strong idea: a ferris wheel that makes the rider older, or younger, depending in which way it turns. This is yet another childhood story, using the familiar situation of children being unable to convince adults of the reality of something they have discovered.[5] It was later expanded into the 1962 novel, *Something Wicked This Way Comes*.

"Fever Dream" (September 1948) was Bradbury's last contribution to *Weird Tales* and also one of his last horror stories. It contains yet another powerful idea, which, as in "Interim," he brings off clumsily. Again the problem is the rationale. A boy, sick in bed, becomes convinced that his hand is no longer his hand. It has ceased to be a part of him. Then the contagion spreads, and he loses his body, bit by bit, until he is a prisoner in something *else*. Then his brain is overwhelmed. It's a hellishly good idea, but Bradbury rationalizes it in terms of mutant germs taking over the body to perpetuate themselves, and this explanation is, in the end, silly.

Bradbury turned away from horror fiction gradually. The sentimental side of his work, which has been present almost from the beginning, became more pronounced. "The Cistern" (published in

Mademoiselle in 1947), for example, is weird enough, a love story about corpses floating around in a sewer, but it *is* a love story, romantic supernaturalism rather than a story of fear.

Then there is a series about a family of Halloween horrors, ghouls, vampires, and the like, but these creatures are not terrifying. They're friendly in their own way, just ordinary folks who happen to drink blood or sleep in coffins. The best of this group, "Homecoming," is about a reunion of the family, and the agonies of a boy who is a "freak" among them—that is, normal. It must have raised eyebrows when published in *Mademoiselle*, even more when it was anthologized in *The Best American Short Stories*. One member of the family, Cecy, a witch who can project her mind over distances, into anyone or anything, is featured in two stories, "The Traveller" (*Weird Tales*, March 1946) and "The April Witch" (*The Saturday Evening Post*, April 5, 1952). These are excellent fantasies, but there is no dread in them.

When Bradbury left *Weird Tales* he turned to more science fiction. He had come into his own there, and, between 1946 and 1950 wrote the stories which made up his famous *The Martian Chronicles*. The early version of *Fahrenheit 451* followed in 1951. Further, he began to sell to the slicks, mass-circulation, high-paying magazines like *Collier's*, *The Saturday Evening Post*, and *Mademoiselle*, which welcomed his mainstream fiction and would sometimes take fantasy or science fiction, but didn't seem to be interested in horror, certainly not stories like "The Handler" or "The Small Assassin."

Undoubtedly, market considerations drew Bradbury away from horror fiction. There was more money and acclaim elsewhere. *Weird Tales*, by the end of the '40s was a minor, failing pulp magazine which paid the lowest rates, hardly of interest to a writer who could sell to *The Saturday Evening Post* or even *Startling Stories*, except for sentimental reasons.

But at the same time, as he matured as a person and as a writer, the Weird Muse departed. His few attempts to return to the horrific mode later in his career have been, for the most part, notable failures. The expansion of "Black Ferris" into *Something Wicked This Way Comes* can only be termed disastrous. The novel is an enormously bloated short story, containing whole chapters in which, in every possible story sense, *nothing happens*. They could have been excised without loss. The characterizations of the two boys have improved, and the added character of Mr. Dark is intriguing, but Bradbury's distinctive style had become, by this point, excessively precious. Truly, the real horror of *Something Wicked* is its prose, with would-be poetry heaped on with a trowel: "Both boys writhed in the iron-maiden clutch of hungry saurians and bristly apes" (p. 244).

Said he mixed-metaphorically.

"The Playground" (*Esquire*, October 1953; included in some editions of *Fahrenheit 451*) attempts to deal with a true childhood horror—the way children bully and torment newcomers, or even the weakest of their own peer group—but it is strangely unmoving. The story is told from the viewpoint of the father, who wants to spare his son these agonies. So, by magic (wishing, really), the son and the father change places. The father, then, is in Hell, among the little monsters. But the adult reader wonders about the son, whose situation is even more grotesque: a six-year old in an adult body, expected to fill an adult's role, of which he knows nothing. This is supposed to be happiness? Bradbury completely ignores the implications.

"Come Into My Cellar" (*Galaxy*, October 1962; collected in *The Machineries of Joy*, 1964) is a childhood paranoia story about children raising mushrooms which are part of an invasion from space, but it is merely clever, a gimmick without any conviction.

Another late story, "The Burning Man" (apparently an original in *Long After Midnight*, 1976) comes closer to the old Bradbury, with its strange hitch-hiker, an old man who carries on about "genetic evil in the world" and how he has risen out of the summer heat and baked mud. He is clearly an uncanny creature, who turns up again as a young boy, who whispers the same line: "— is there such a thing as genetic evil in the world?"

The problem is that the story is not about genetics. Bradbury has chosen the wrong word, and diluted his climax.

His talent did not so much vanish as turn elsewhere. The title story in *Long After Midnight* (first published as "The Long-After-Midnight Girl" in *Eros*, Winter 1962) shows all the old brilliance, and even has a beginning which seems to suggest a horror story:

> The police ambulance went up into the palisades at the wrong hour. It is always the wrong hour when the police ambulance goes anywhere, but this was especially wrong, for it was long after midnight and nobody imagined it would be day again, because the sea coming in on the lightless shore said as much and the wind blowing salt cold in from the Pacific reaffirmed this, and the fog muffling the sky and putting out the stars struck the final, unfelt-but-disabling blow. The weather said it had been here forever, man was hardly here at all, and would soon be gone. (p.251)

The ambulance crew finds what seems to be a woman's corpse dangling from a branch on a lonely clifftop, and as they drive down they speculate, brutally and voyeuristically, about the sadnesses and tragedies which drove the woman to suicide. Then, at the end, they discover that it's the corpse of a transvestite, and the horror, and the story's impact, comes from the realization that the tragedy is just as real, for all that everyone's prejudices need readjusting.

Bradbury, late in his career, has excelled at this sort of story, as his science fiction has grown weaker and his horror fiction has vanished altogether. (A final story *Weird Tales* subjects, "The Wish," published in *Woman's Day* in 1973, is sentimental.) Possibly this is because life continues to inspire him, but he has had no fresh inspiration in science fiction or fantasy in nearly forty years. And he has exhausted the old material. Also, he is much farther away from childhood now, and probably could not write something like "The Emissary" as easily in his sixties as he could at twenty-three.

His importance as a writer of horror fiction stems entirely from the first ten years of his career. It can be summed up with the stories in *The October Country*, which is, to some extent, a re-edited version of *Dark Carnival*. Bradbury has always been a capable judge of his own fiction. Most of the stories he dropped when compiling *The October Country* (like "Interim") were indeed inferior to the new material he was adding. The stories he never collected at all, for the most part, deserve neglect.

Great writing in any field has never been something to be judged by the pound. Quantity is not the point. Bradbury's great stories—"The Next in Line," "Skeleton," "The Jar," "The Emissary," "The Small Assassin," "The Crowd," "The Scythe," "The Wind," "The Man Upstairs," "There Was an Old Woman," and a very few others opened the way for numerous subsequent writers. They are classics, in every sense of the word, and will assure the author's lasting fame alongside Poe, Lovecraft, Blackwood, Machen, M.R. James, and the other masters of the supernatural horror story.

The important point is not that he wrote a few great stories early in his career, then failed to follow them up, but that he wrote them at all.

NOTES

1. Moskowitz's *Horrors Unknown*, published by Walker in 1971, contains both versions.
2. Clear allusions to "The Crowd," "Undersea Guardians" (a weak wartime fantasy about a U-boat, published in *Amazing* in 1944), "The Emissary" (dogs), "The Wind," and "There Was an Old Woman," all of which must have been written, or at least contemplated by this time. There is no specific train story, but the image of the train is put to good use in the opening of *Something Wicked This Way Comes*.
3. Indeed, for all the creation of E.C. Comics was still some years in the future, Bradbury and E.C. Comics were made for each other. At the very time he was being praised by the ever-conservative literary establishment as a major American writer, his stories were being

adapted into those horror comics parents were trying to burn and ban. A selection of these adaptions can be found in two paperbacks, *The Autumn People* (Ballantine, 1965)' and *Tomorrow Midnight* (Ballantine, 1966).

4. He reputedly has a sign over his writing desk that says: DON'T THINK! The idea is that his stories are supposed to be pure, emotional outbursts. But obviously this technique has its pitfalls.

5. Examples: in "The Trunk Lady" it's a body in a trunk, in "The Screaming Woman," the still-living wife of a neighbor, buried in a rubbish heap; in "The Man Upstairs," the landlady's boy discovers that the new boarder is a vampire, and isn't believed, even after he starts a dissection; it is one of the most basic childish nightmare/fantasies, to be the only one who *knows* about some horror, and unable to convince anyone else.

BIBLIOGRAPHY

Dark Carnival. Arkham House, 1947. Contains: "The Homecoming," "Skeleton," "The Jar," "The Lake," "The Maiden," "The Tombstone," "The Smiling People," "The Emissary," "The Traveller," "The Small Assassin," "The Crowd," "Reunion," "The Handler," "The Coffin," "Interim," "Jack-in-the-Box," "The Scythe," "Let's Play Poison," "Uncle Einar," "The Wind," "The Night," "There Was an Old Woman," "The Dead Man," "The Man Upstairs," "The Night Sets," "The Cistern," "The Next in Line."

The October Country. Ballantine, 1955. Contains: "The Dwarf," "The Next in Line," "The Watchful Poker Chip of H. Matisse," "Skeleton," "The Jar," "The Lake," "The Emissary," "Touched With Fire," "The Small Assassin," "The Crowd," "Jack-in-the-Box," "The Scythe," "Uncle Einar," "The Wind," "The Man Upstairs," "There Was an Old Woman," "The Cistern," "Homecoming," "The Wonderful Death of Dudley Stone."

A Memory of Murder. Dell, 1984. Contains: "The Small Assassin," "A Careful Man Dies," "It Burns Me Up!" "Half-Pint Homicide," "Four-Way Funeral," "The Long Night," "Corpse Carnival," "Hell's Half Hour," "The Long Way Home," "Wake for the Living," (the same as "The Coffin"), "'I'm Not So Dumb!'" "The Trunk Lady," "Yesterday I Lived," "Dead Men Rise Up Never," "The Candy Skull."

Bloch and Bradbury. Tower Books, 1969. Material by Robert Bloch, plus the following stories by Bradbury: "The Watchers," "Fever Dream," "The Handler," "The Dead Man."

Something Wicked This Way Comes. Simon and Schuster, 1962.

Uncollected stories in *Weird Tales*:
"The Candle," November 1942
"The Ducker," September 1943
"The Sea Shell," January 1944
"Bang! You're Dead!" September 1944
"The Poems," January 1945
"The Black Ferris," May 1946

"The Screaming Woman," *Today*, May 27, 1951. Collected in *S Is for Space*, Doubleday, 1966.

THE POETICS OF THE UNCONSCIOUS: THE "STRANGE STORIES" OF ROBERT AICKMAN

By Gary William Crawford

Robert Aickman is a unique figure in modern supernatural horror fiction.[1] Unlike such writers as Lovecraft, Bloch, King, and Straub, Aickman is subtle, haunting, and, above all, poetic. His "strange stories," as he preferred to call them, are essentially symbolic and metaphorical. Frequently in Aickman's work, it is possible to discern a confrontation, not only by the protagonist of the tale and by the reading mind, but by the work itself as a coherent work of art, with unconscious contents.

Aickman's works are unified by a coherent structure which contains metaphor and symbol, and as in a poem, there is an inner tension that is allegorical—as in symbol and metaphor. Aickman is thus certainly unique, but if he resembles any writer, he is closest to Walter de la Mare. The most striking resemblance between the art of de la Mare and that of Aickman lies in their creation of what Peter Penzoldt calls "the inconclusive tale of terror."[2] The technique of such a tale consists in the writer's suggesting "a supernatural danger lurking directly behind our back, or just outside the range of our five senses, but ready at any moment to pounce upon its victim."[3] In such stories as de la Mare's "Seaton's Aunt," "A Recluse," and "Out of the Deep," the supernatural never appears in any outward manifestation. Similarly, in Aickman's fiction, the supernatural possibilities, if not actualities, grow out of character development naturally, and much like the symbolism and metaphor in poetry, carry the meaning of the stories. Rarely does Aickman write about traditional ghost, werewolf, or vampire (the vampire tale "Pages from a Young Girl's Journal" is an exception), but he evokes an uncanny realm of implicit terror, violence, and death, always counterpoised by human love. Aickman, even in his darkest fictions, conceives of a humanity that can achieve insight into its infections of the soul, even though, frequently, it means willful entrance into those realms. As Aickman has written, the supernatural tale is "allied to poetry."[4]

Above all, Aickman's life and works express a reverence for mystery, or what the Germans call *Ehrfurct*: reverence for what one cannot understand. He thus aligns himself with Sigmund Freud, who in his *Civilization and Its Discontents* speaks most clearly of the concerns expressed on Aickman's art. Like Freud, Aickman revered the unknowable; and all of his stories place his characters, and the reader by extension, in touch with the vast realm of the unconscious. Not only do his stories express such a confrontation, but Aickman's entire life may be called poetic.

I

Robert Fordyce Aickman was born in London in 1915, the son of W.A. Aickman. He was the grandson of Richard Marsh, popular novelist, who authored the supernatural horror novel *The Beetle*. In Aickman's autobiography *The Attempted Rescue*[5] one is struck by the oddity of his father, who was fifty-three when he married. His bride was twenty-three. Aickman had a very odd upbringing, as is detailed in his autobiography. If any passage from *The Attempted Rescue* sums up the philosophy Aickman acquired, it is the opening one:

> In the end I came to see that the true prophet of the modern world was Samuel Butler: when he suggested that the machine was an evolutionary development destined to supersede man as the dominant species and reduce him to greenfly status, the status of machine-minder, homo mechanicus instead of homo sapiens; and to modify his nature accordingly.[6]

His entire life may be seen as a reaction to this condition of modern man, for he early became interested in art, drama, ballet, literature, and nature. He received some training as an architect, and in his twenties, he aspired to be an author. At the beginning of the war, he met and married Ray Gregorson, and he became fascinated with the supernatural, as, in 1943, he spent a night in the famous haunted Borley Rectory with Ray.[7]

His interest in preserving nature was expressed most dramatically by his foundation in 1946 of The Inland Waterways Association. He wrote two popular books on the subject of British waterways, *The Story of Our Inland Waterways* and *Know Your Waterways.*[8] His enthusiasm was infectious, and The Inland Waterways Association now has a very large membership.

Aickman's dedication to the performing arts was prodigious, as he was dramatic critic to *The Nineteenth Century and After*, film critic to *The Jewish Monthly*, chairman from 1954 to 1969 of The London Opera Society, and he was connected with the famous Ballets Minerva. He was director of The 1950 Market Harborough Festival of Boats and Arts, which was attended by an estimated fifty thousand visitors.

Aickman was thus a many-sided man, and his dedication to the Romantic reaction to the industrial age is expressed in his fiction. He had many discontents, from all reports, and he must have suffered privately, as his wife Ray divorced him in 1957 after a religious experience and entered an Anglican nunnery. Some, particularly his men friends, have said that he was often not an easy man with whom to relate. A few of his friends and acquaintances found him overbearing, and few could share his interest in the supernatural.

His philosophy of life is clearly reflected in his fictioh, and in 1981, when he died after a long illness, he had produced some fifty stories of the weird, and he left a large number of people devoted to him, despite his flaws, or rather, his discontents with modern civilization.

II

Above all, Aickman's private discontents compelled him to look to "a world elsewhere," as Coriolanus put it. He revered the mystery that courses under modern civilization, and he found in nature and the arts causes for which he could fight. As Christine Pasanen Morris points out in reference to Aickman's fictional characters:

> They are natural products of their societies, up-bringings, and consciences. Aickman knows, however, that an unremarkable appearance may cover a surprising interior of memories, hidden dreams and repressed or suppressed frustrations, angers, and urges. Despite the rein of the ego or the superego, the mind may call up hidden things into existence. Are they real or are they only imagined? Either way, the experiences are vivid and real to the one who experiences them.[9]

It is largely this interior of memories and dreams which rise to the surface in the "inconclusive" manner of de la Mare. Aickman's stories are, in this respect, odd and poetic and symbolic: they acquaint the reader with the hidden wellsprings of the unconscious that courses under the surface.

An example of Aickman's "poetry of the unconscious" is to be found in one of his first published stories, "The Trains," which appeared in the Christmas 1951 issue of *The Tatler*. In this tale, two girls on a hiking trip find refuge at a country house near a railroad line; the constant passing of the trains seems to symbolize the confused mental states of the two girls. The world of the country house, with its lonely master and the strange woman who may or may not be a ghost (Aickman never overtly says she is), is unstable and terrifying. The two girls who enter this realm are faced with an uncanny series of events that have no rational explanation. As in all of Aickman's stories, nothing is resolved in any logical way. The stories themselves, their events and characters, seem about to explode into time and space. There is, however, a dream-like logic, which is the reader's direct confrontation with unconscious contents.

There is, perhaps, a more clear confrontation with the unconscious in "The View," in which Carfax, a middle-aged bachelor recovering from a long illness, travels to an island in the Irish Sea, where he comes upon a mansion owned by a mysterious and beautiful woman who has no name. Carfax names her, however, Ariel. Carfax is a painter, and while staying in Ariel's home, he attempts to paint a seascape that continually changes, just as Carfax himself changes. When Carfax returns from the island, he has become a very old man. Here, the changing view Carfax attempts to paint symbolizes the shifting, contradictory nature of time, and quotations from Matthew Arnold, Walter Pater, and Thomas Beddoes, convey a sense of implicit violence and death.

"Ringing the Changes," which has been filmed for television, displays a surface that is realistic, but undermined by psychic unease, as an older man and his considerably younger bride (a couple that may be modeled after Aickman's own parents) honeymoon at a seaside town. As in all of Aickman's tales, the characters find themselves in an apparently normal world that becomes stranger as the story progresses. Throughout "Ringing the Changes," church bells are continually ringing; the town in which the couple honeymoon seems strangely backward; and eventually the two learn, to their horror, that the changes are being rung by the townspeople to wake the dead—literally. Aickman equates marriage with death in the tale: indeed, love and death are mated.

Love and death expressed as symbols of unconscious darkness are to be found in "Choice of Weapons" as well. The main character, Malcolm Fenville, learns of the terror of love when he falls in love at first sight with Dorabelle, who lives alone in the house of her dead parents. Dorabelle leads Malcolm on, but later reveals that she is in love with and will marry an eighteenth century gentleman she has met in the supernatural mirror in her room. Malcolm comes under the influence, meanwhile, of Dr. Bermuda, who says that he will cure Malcolm of love. Eventually, Malcolm encounters Dorabelle's eighteenth century fiancee in her house and duels with him, his choice of weapons being a rapier. Malcolm kills the man, only to discover that he has killed Dorabelle. Bermuda, an ominous presence throughout this mysterious tale, arrives and says that he has failed to cure Malcolm.

The story reads like a dream, and no rational explanation is ever offered. The supernatural mirror in Dorabelle's room seems to symbolize the unconscious itself, and Dorabelle herself may or may not be a figment of Malcolm's imagination. Dr. Bermuda is like a psychologist, a doctor of the soul, and when Malcolm kills Dorabelle, Bermuda is like Charon, who carries Malcolm to the other side of the Styx, to that endless night of unconscious.

"Bind Your Hair" is another example of the "inconclusive" technique Aickman utilizes so often. In its strange suggestiveness of a supernatural rapport between a bride-to-be and the leader of a mysterious cult, it suggests a direct confrontation with unconscious "sympathy of souls," or what Carl Jung, the famous student of Freud, called "synchronicity," an acausal connecting principle common in certain forms of mental illness. Clarinda, the bride-to-be, goes to visit her fiancee's family in the country. She feels an outsider with them, and on a foggy night, she ventures out into the countryside to the home of Mrs. Pagani, a neighbor, and there she witnesses a strange and utterly inexplicable ritual that symbolizes her unconscious fears about her impending marriage.

Often in Aickman's fiction, a character's confrontation with his own unconscious fears is also a confrontation with mystery: the things one cannot understand. An example of such is "The Inner Room," in which a woman narrates her early childhood with her struggling family, which later splits apart. She receives as a birthday gift an enormous dollhouse which is a source of almost supernatural mystery for her because it contains an inaccessible inner room. Later in life, in a curious episode, she visits what is apparently the actual house after which the dollhouse was modeled and comes close to discovering a nameless horror in the inner room. That inner room poetically signifies the hidden life of dream, or rather dream as reality, which we repress, much to our emotional peril.

Occasionally, love and death, as was mentioned before, figures in Aickman's stories. Love is the purifying flame; and death the uncanny realm of implicit violence and terror. Love, even sexual love, is a pointed theme in "Ravissante." This tale is actually a tale within a tale, as the first narrator relates his acquaintance with a painter of bizarre and surreal subjects. The painter is a bachelor, and he leaves to a friend a manuscript in which he narrates his visit to another painter, a Madame A., who ravishes him with a kind of ghostly sexuality that leaves him marked for life.

"Marriage" is an even better example of the bizarre sexuality which becomes a source of the weird in Aickman's fiction. It concerns a young man who loves two women, one blonde and shy and staid, the other dark and voluptuous, free in her sexuality. The two women are perhaps clear Freudian types, and, inspired by Freud, Aickman has his young man unable to decide between the two women, and, horror of horrors, the young man ends up in bed with his mother, whom he truly loves.

A much stronger and stranger uncanny flavor is exemplified in "Into the Wood." As Christine Pasanen Morris points out in her study of female characters in Aickman's works:

> Margaret...encounters guests at the Jamblichus Kurhus who at first seem merely to be eccentric recluses. The more time she spends there, though, the more and more unreal they become—more and more like the undead or souls trapped in a limbo of their constant and unearthly insomnia.[10]

Margaret Sawyer desires something greater than what husband and family offer, and she forsakes the world of the suburbs of Manchester and goes "into the wood" at the Jamblichus Kurhus. Her final decision to remain at the Kurhus even after learning that willful entrance into that world means death for some of the patients, as they walk the woods without sleeping, takes on the quality of a descent into the unconscious; but for Margaret it is a descent motivated by love for something greater, and perhaps, more honest, than the stifling life she leads with her husband.

Similarly, in "Pages from a Young Girl's Journal," a young girl feels alienated from her family and the nineteenth century society in which she lives. As Christine Pasanen Morris writes, she "retreats more and more from the world of her family and other mortals to become one of the undead elect, a vampire, who has nothing but distant scorn for mortal values and perceptions."[11]

Other stories like these repeatedly fuse poetry and fiction and develop characters who are jaded by the modern world and come to know the utter mystery at the heart of their lives. "The Clock Watcher" is another symbolic fable of a man whose wife collects clocks of all sorts. His wife seems to become more absorbed into time and space, and the clocks become almost malignant living things that destroy her and carry her off into an unconscious realm. Time as another world of illusion also figures in "No Time Is Passing" as a man enters another world across a river where time itself is meaningless.

It is precisely this metaphorical and symbolic technique which hints at a timeless, psychosymbolical world in Aickman's fiction. Reality and the civilization that supports it is only an illusion, and Aickman is aware, like Freud, of the rich and poetic symbolism of dream—the true life of the unconscious.

III

As the above examples of Aickman's stories reveal, their mere plot incidents and themes are undeniably odd and, more importantly, poetic. Jack Sullivan has remarked, "With its exquisitely shaded ambiguities, precisely tuned diction, and bell-like musicality, Aickman's work is consummately 'poetic,' a triumphant rejoinder to the notion that the ghost story as an art is dead."[12] He is, in this respect, a unique voice in supernatural horror fiction since the 1950s. In other respects, Aickman resembles Leiber more closely than he does any other writer. For example, the poetry of the climax of Leiber's *Our Lady of Darkness* wells from the same springs of the unconscious one finds in Aickman's art. Indeed, Leiber has called Aickman "the weatherman of the unconscious," and this is certainly true. Yet some of Ramsey Campbell's short stories resemble Aickman's poetic artistry in that, like Aickman, Campbell often refuses to explain his stories away, as in "Drawing In" and "The Christmas Present." The ghost is not banished, but, in Aickman, lingers in the reader's mind long afterward, and his stories can be reread with increasing pleasure.

Some readers complain that Aickman is too obscure in that there is so much in his stories that is unstated. But Aickman, in his collection of stories *Cold Hand in Mine*, draws his epigraph from Sachaverell Sitwell: "In the end it is the mystery that lasts and not the explanation." It is utter mystery that Aickman reveres, and surely his works present a coherent philosophy, like the works of H.P. Lovecraft.

Aickman's stories may be somewhat obscure, but they are, like Lovecraft's, assuredly timeless, the true test of great art. One wonders, as one compares Aickman to such a writer as the phenomenally successful Stephen King, which writer will survive the longest. Aikman will very likely survive longer because he creates a timeless world in the reader's mind. Unlike King, Aickman does not pander to popular taste or fashion, and there is nothing crude of vulgar about Aickman. This coherent philosophy, or rather, outlook, this care for detail and timeless awe, or rather, mystery, will allow Aickman to rise above King and the large numbers of horror novelists and short story writers we find at the present time.

If Aickman's stories are in any way flawed, there are times when his "unconscious poetry" is flaccid, not as forceful as it should be. An example of an Aickman story that fails is "Residents Only." Even "Growing Boys," which Aickman regarded as one of his best stories, fails because the metaphor becomes funny rather than uncanny.

Aickman lamented, in his last year, the fact that his stories could not be easily described as Gothic, or as horror stories at all, and that, commercially, he suffered from this.[13]

However, in the final analysis, it is very likely that Aickman's works may become masterpieces of weird fiction. His achievement will only be fully assessed in time as his life and works are studied in depth and placed in perspective. Still, he is certainly a unique voice in modern terror fiction. He revered the mysterious, the inexplicable, the surprising, the uncanny, and wrote about this reverence in a delicate, haunting, and poetic manner. Aickman was, in short, a master at what he chose to do—write "strange stories."

NOTES

1. This essay selectively surveys Aickman's published work to 1 September 1983.
2. Peter Penzoldt, *The Supernatural in Fiction* (New York: Humanities Press, 1965), p.203.
3. Penzoldt, p.205.
4. *The Fontana Book of Great Ghost Stories* (London: Fontana, 1964), p.7.
5. (London: Gollancz, 1966).
6. *The Attempted Rescue*, p.7.
7. See Harry Price, *The End of Borley Rectory* (London: Harrap, 1946), pp.75-77, and Eric J. Dingwall, Kathleen M. Goldney, and Trevor H. Hall, *The Haunting of Borley Rectory* (London: Duckworth, 1956), p.150.
8. (London: Pitman, 1955) and (London: Coram, 1955).
9. "The Female Outsider in the Short Fiction of Robert Aickman," *Nyctalops*, No. 18 (1983), p.56.
10. "The Female Outsider," p.58.
11. Ibid.
12. Jack Sullivan, ed., *Lost Souls: A Collection of English Ghost Stories* (Athens: Ohio University Press, 1983), p.373.
13. Letter received from Robert Aickman dated 25 February 1980.

BIBLIOGRAPHY

Compiled by Darrell Schweitzer

Dark Entries. Collins, London, 1964.
Powers of Darkness. Collins, London, 1966.
Sub Rosa: Strange Tales. Gollancz, London 1968.
Cold Hand in Mine. Scribners, New York, 1975.
Tales of Love and Death. Gollancz, London, 1977.
Painted Devils. Scribners, New York, 1979.
Intrusions. Gollancz, London, 1980.
Night Voices. Gollancz, London, 1985.

By Robert Aickman and Elizabeth Jane Howard:

We Are for the Dark: Six Ghost Stories. Jonathon Cape, London, 1951.

MICHAEL McDOWELL AND
THE HAUNTED SOUTH
By Michael E. Stamm

When one considers American horror fiction in geographical terms, several areas come to mind. There are the New England tales of H.P. Lovecraft, Peter Straub, Stephen King and Charles Grant; the North Carolina and Tennessee stories of Manly Wade Wellman and Karl Edward Wagner; the midwestern tales of Tom Reamy; the southwestern stories of Robert E. Howard, and the southern California nightmares of Dennis Etchison. And there are, of course, other possibilities.

One of those other areas is, naturally, the South. Not so much starting at the Mason-Dixon Line; like a state boundary, that's a border that is a metaphor for something, but standing on it things don't look really different on either side. But the further south you go, past Kentucky and Tennessee and on into Mississippi and Louisiana, Alabama and Georgia, the character of out-of-the-way corners of the landscape and their inhabitants tends to feel stranger and stranger.

It is from the South that the stories of William Faulkner come, stories like "A Rose for Emily," which avoided the supernatural entirely but is chilling all the same. Here too we find writers like Carson McCullers and Flannery O'Connor, who in stories like "The Ballad of the Sad Cafe" and "Good Country People" portrayed landscapes and created people in forgotten backwaters and on lonely farms outre enough for a Poe or Lovecraft; James Dickey, whose *Deliverance* told of a lawless ferocity and perversion hard to imagine elsewhere; Katherine Anne Porter, who in stories like "Noon Wine" creates unforgettable atmospheres of isolation and hidden violence; Tennessee Williams, who went from early stories like "Desire and the Black Masseur" to dark dramas like *The Glass Menagerie*; and Eudora Welty, whose *Delta Wedding* has no ghosts or horrors but an atmosphere harkening back to a mythic, almost pre-human pastoralism, and who is the only regional writer to have noticeably influenced Michael McDowell.

Though he has not yet attained the stature of these other writers, Michael McDowell is in some respects very much in their tradition. Born in southeastern Alabama in 1950, he has published five novels and a six-volume series novel—not counting the four others he has written in collaboration with a friend—since 1979.[1] McDowell spent most of his early life in the deep South, in towns and among people very much like the towns and people of Perdido, Pine Cone, and Babylon that appear in his stories. He went north to attend college, entering Harvard in 1968 and ultimately receiving a Ph.D. in 1978 from Brandeis University. Having decided well before that that he did not want to teach, and having a half-dozen unsold novels to his credit, he had a fairly good idea of what he wanted to do instead.

The Amulet was sold to Avon Books in 1977 and, after considerable expansion, was published in 1979. McDowell's first horror novel, it could almost be described as a "splatter" novel, were it not for his ingenuity at methods of mayhem and his taste for very black humor.

The Amulet takes place in 1965, in and around Pine Cone, Alabama, on the edge of what is called the Wiregrass region in the southeastern corner of the state. Pine Cone itself is carefully described, with a care and an eye for detail reminiscent of the description of Stephen King's Jerusalem's Lot.

The Amulet is the story of Dean Howell, Vietnam-bound draftee who loses most of his face in a graphically described accident with a defective rifle—built in his home town of Pine Cone—and spends almost all of the novel as a silent, motionless, bandaged presence in the darkness of his mother's home; of his wife Sarah, who is the nearest thing to a protagonist the novel has; his mother Jo, who unleashes the amulet's murderous power in her vicious rage against the town whose sole industry maimed her son; and the dozen or so residents of Pine Cone who lose their lives in violent but imaginative ways in the course of the novel.

The story line of The Amulet can only be called a plot in the most generous terms. It started with the idea of a possessed child with the unlikely name of Fred, who didn't make it to the final draft, and the novel doubled in length not once but twice before it was published. It is essentially a sequence of gruesome, violent deaths connected by the sketchiest of plots.

The origin of the amulet itself—a three-inch gold-rimmed disc of jet, on a chain with no visible fastening—is never explained; there is no indication of where the thing comes from, or how or why it does what it apparently does. This is something that recurs in McDowell's later work; there is often an object, or a person, or a place, that seems to be the focus or the source of strange and irrational forces, but it is a function of McDowell's assertion of that very irrationality that what seems to be—for lack of any better explanation—is not always the case.

Jo Howell first gives the amulet to a neighbor whose family owns the factory which made the rifle that injured her son; the neighbor gives it to his wife, who inadvertently puts it on—and proceeds to apparently poison her husband and five children and set fire to their home, and sits on her bed dandling a suffocating infant while her house and family burn to death around her in a ghastly conflagration that will kill her as well.

The amulet is found afterwards in the ruins, unharmed, by the daughter of a policeman; she gives it to her mother, who also accidentally puts it on, and murders her husband by thrusting an icepick through his ear into his brain and is kept from killing her daughter only when she trips and cuts her own throat on a shard of broken mirror. From there the amulet passes to the dead man's sister, who forces her husband to drive their car off a bridge into a river, where she beats him to death; she is killed by a truck while trying to return to the highway. The driver of the truck finds the amulet and gives it to his wife, who drops it into a pigsty and is torn apart by the pigs when she tries to retrieve it. And the amulet continues to pass from hand to hand, and those who find it come to violent ends—shot to death, mangled or crushed in machinery, decapitated, even agitated to death in a washing machine. The story comes to full circle when Sarah Howell—who has had increasing suspicions about the amulet from the first, and has been gradually working out the chain of circumstance connecting the deaths, for which the amulet provides the only links—escapes a holocaust at the rifle factory, a catastrophe in which her best friend and many others die horribly and in which the amulet itself may have been destroyed. She returns home to her husband and his mother—and as the novel ends she has done him in and is almost certainly going to kill her mother-in-law as well.

Like some of McDowell's later books, *The Amulet* is something of a curiosity. The tone is matter-of-fact and so, in certain circumstances, very funny; the characters, especially the women, often do not act in anything resembling a logical manner, but in the context of the story their words and deeds seem oddly appropriate. For the experienced horror reader there seem to be many lost opportunities for making the story more complex and frightening than it already is; but there is something indefinably compelling about the novel, in a sense of McDowell's awareness of the general ridiculousness of life which transcends the clinical descriptions of horrifying violence in a way that leaves the tale perversely entertaining without being truly perverse.

In the hidden workings of *The Amulet*, the supernatural was implied but never explicitly evoked. In *Cold Moon Over Babylon*—published not quite a year later, in 1980—McDowell uses the supernatural in a much more overt—if no more explained—fashion.

The story takes place, again, in the deep South—this time slightly further south, in and around the town of Babylon, on the Styx River in the Florida panhandle. Babylon, like Pine Cone, if it is not real—and I can't find it in my atlas—is modeled on real Southern small towns. *Cold Moon Over Babylon* is another story of vengeance, this time a contemporary tale of retribution from beyond the grave. Young

Margaret Larkin is murdered by a mysterious assailant, her mutilated body bound to her bicycle and sunk in the black waters of the Styx—a river also not in my atlas but whose name can be no coincidence—the river where her parents disappeared forever from their boat five years before. Her body is finally found, and an autopsy reveals that she had been pregnant at the time of her death; but before much of an attempt to find her killer is made, her brother and grandmother are also murdered by the same man. The killer is revealed as the wastrel son of the town banker, who has taken over management of the bank from his ailing father but tends to spend or gamble away more money than even he can make. He had raped Margaret Larkin, and murdered her when she informed him she was pregnant and that he would have to do right by her; having acquired a taste for violence, he killed her brother and grandmother to end their suspicions and to clear the way for his acquisition of their berry farm, suspected to be located over rich oil-fields.

But he is not to escape unpunished. *Something* rises from the impenetrable depths of the Styx; something haunting him, hunting him, dripping from the shadowed branches overhead in uninhabited pine forests, leaving handprints in river silt on his car, something made apparently entirely of water, with eyes blacker and colder than the endless gulfs of space.

Cold Moon Over Babylon, like its predecessor, is not to be looked to for impeccable logic or certifiable cause-and-effect, even in supernatual forces. As McDowell expresses later in *The Elementals* (1981), one of the most terrifying things about the supernatural is that it need not behave in logical ways, that it can be utterly malevolent but unpredictable and inconsistent as well. The ghosts, or whatever they are, of *Cold Moon Over Babylon* are bent on vengeance—but they do not always behave as traditional ghosts would behave. There are many novels which are more successful as artistic wholes, but *Cold Moon* has some of the most terrifying scenes ever put on paper. In one the town sheriff, at the deserted Larkin house looking for Margaret's brother and grandmother, hears "a noise behind him, in the kitchen—a soft wet slap, as of a sodden sponge falling to the floor...A tiny naked arm, gray and wet, dangled over the edge of the sink. The slender fingers unclutched slowly out of a fist as it slowly drew back into the basin" and flees in terror (p. 180). In another the killer is lured, almost in a dream state, late at night into the cemetery where his victims are buried, and sees—not knowing if it is a dream or reality—the coffins tearing themselves from the earth and being burst from within by the restless dead.

The novel ends with the killer's phantasmagorical battle with and flight from the three awful spectres, a battle in which he accidentally murders his own brother and a flight which ends in his nightmarish death at the bottom of the Styx. *Cold Moon Over Babylon* is probably McDowell's most frightening novel so far. It shows distinct improvements over *The Amulet*, with a much sounder plot and a more solid understanding of the horror writer's craft.

Gilded Needles appeared only seven months later, in November of 1980. It is a historical novel, growing out of work related to research McDowell had done for his doctoral dissertation—on death in America, 1825-1865—and is more complex than either of the novels preceding it. It is crafted with great care and filled with an extraordinary amount of historical detail. *Gilded Needles*—the title refers to the *yen hock*, the needle used by opium addicts, which appears in its normal role and as a particularly unpleasant murder weapon—has probably the least humor of any of McDowell's novels so far; it is a fascinating but often depressingly grim tale.

The novel is set in 19th century New York, encompassing the entire year of 1882, mostly in that part of the city once known as the Black Triangle, an appalling crime- and vice-ridden slum whose description is similar to accounts of London's East End—the haunt of Jack the Ripper—at about the same time.

McDowell has said that revenge is an important emotion in human life but one which only works satisfactorily in books, where all factors can be controlled. In *Gilded Needles* the story is, yet again, one of revenge: the revenge of Black Lena Shanks and her criminal family and friends against Judge James Stallworth and his family, in retaliation for the judge's pitiless persecution of members of the Shanks family. At the judge's order Black Lena spent long years in prison, and her husband was hanged; not long after the novel begins, a close friend of the Shanks family commits suicide rather than go to the prison where she has been unjustly sentenced as a casualty of a Stallworth campaign for political office, and one of the Shanks daughters is murdered in a brawl with police. The novel chronicles the careful moves made by the Shanks family against the Stallworths—and the careless moves, made in pride and arrogance by the Stallworths, that play into their enemies' hands. The midpoint of the novel sees four members of the Shanks family dead; by the end, two of the Stallworths are dead by violence, three more are lost to their family forever, and one may be permanently mad.

Gilded Needles is a big and impressive book, darkly Dickensian in its scope and complexity. In it McDowell expands on his recurring theme of the family as an institution of enormous and not always beneficial influence on its members and the people around it. It also demonstrates McDowell's lack of concern with social definitions of good and evil; though ostensibly evil, the Shanks family is so largely through no fault of its own, and is capable of good; though ostensibly good, the Stallworth's are capable—and guilty—of great evil. *Gilded Needles* is a novel of entirely human horror. It is also a product of McDowell's continuing interest in all aspects of nineteenth-century life—and death; an interest which shows to advantage in the extraordinarily rich texture of the novel, and to which McDowell will return again.

Eleven months later, in October 1981, McDowell published *The Elementals*, which returns to the realm of the supernatural for much of its power. It is to date McDowell's personal favorite, embodying both the Southern "extravagance of speech" (and to some extent of action) he has adopted from the writings of Eudora Welty (an extravagance which will be even more apparent in the massive, multi-volume novel *Blackwater* [1983]) and the kinds of horror closest to his own heart. These last were ideas, and sometimes unplanned scenes, that sometimes frightened him to the point where he had to stop writing them.

The Elementals is the story of the Savage and McCray families. It opens with the funeral of matriarch Marian Savage, where her son Dauphin and daughter Big Barbara McCray perform one of the most outre rituals in modern horror fiction by stabbing their mother's corpse to ensure her death. Most of the story takes place at Beldame, a set of three Savage-owned summer houses on a sandspit—which becomes an island at high tide—in the Gulf of Mexico. The elementals of the title are monstrous forces—said to haunt the uninhabited third house which is slowly being engulfed by sand, but actually able to be anywhere—lurking in the Beldame shadows and slowly but surely growing on power over the years. The elementals manifest themselves in various ways—as footsteps, with no signs of anything to make them; as the dead Marian Savage; as shapes of living sand; as a little black girl who was washed out into the Gulf and drowned years before. Only the family's black housekeeper has any notion of what the elementals are and how they work—that is, that they are inhuman and malevolent, behaving according to no human laws or understanding—and in the end her knowledge does not save her. With the two oldest living men of the Savage and McCray families, she dies in an onslaught of elemental evil that turns into a fire destroying the doomed third house; later that year, in a final stroke by an uncaring fate, the two remaining houses of Beldame are utterly destroyed in a hurricane.

The Elementals in its various sections is by turns very funny—as with the larger-than-life but somehow believable Savage and McCray family squabbles—and very frightening, ranging in degree from the image of the three out-of-place mansions in their bleak setting by the Gulf to the manifestations of the elementals, invisibly shutting disused doors or appearing as apparitions of the long dead. The precocious India McCray's exploration of the long-abandoned third house culminates in a scene seldom rivaled for nightmarish imagery. "As [India] pressed the shutter, the prone figure of sand sat suddenly up. The sand on her breast and head fell quickly away. It was a little grinning black girl....The Negro child pawed up the dune to the window and lifted her black face to stare into India's. Sand welled in the corners of her white-pupiled black eyes. She opened her mouth to laugh, but no sound, only a long ribbon of white dry sand spilled out of it" (p.109).

As a whole *The Elementals* does not succeed artistically on the level of *Cold Moon Over Babylon*, though it is not for want of trying; perhaps the plot is too alien to the tradition of cause-and-effect, even in the supernatural, more common in American horror fiction. McDowell's use of the theme of the malevolent, the unpredictable, the absolutely non-human as supernatural force is an important one, and in terms of fears touches many a hidden nerve; its lack of total success may lie in the implication that there are destructive and uncaring forces Out There, and there is nothing we can do about them. In a sense this puts such forces on a level with natural disasters like earthquakes and hurricanes, forces so alien to humans and so uncontrollable that to worry about them in the abstract is a waste of time and to hope to combat them in actuality is futile. *The Elementals* continues to demonstrate McDowell's ability with scenes of real horror, and allows him to work more with usually normal elements—water in *Cold Moon*, sand in *The Elementals*—as foci for the images of fear.

McDowell continued his consistently prolific schedule with *Katie*, published in September, 1981. *Katie* is, after a fashion, a return to the nineteenth-century world of *Gilded Needles*; it is McDowell's second historical crime/horror novel, set for the most part in New Jersey and New York in 1871. Considering that the title character is an uneducated clairvoyant and murderess, the novel has a comparatively light tone; it has the density of detail and convincing atmosphere, without much of the overwhelming grimness, of *Gilded Needles*.

The prologue to the story introduces the reader to the young but already psychopathic Katie Slape in Philadelphia in 1863, sitting with a woman—soon to be Katie's stepmother—learning the unpleasant profession of stunting puppies with forced doses of cheap gin to sell them to self-indulgent rich women. The novel itself begins eight years later in New Egypt, New Jersey, with the trials and tribulations of young Philo Drax, the intrepid young woman who is really the main character of the story and after whom the book should have been named.

The plot is rather straightforward. Philo leaves her impecunious mother to visit her wealthy grandfather, with whom her mother has had no contact for many years, to find that he has been swindled out of his farm by John and Hannah Jepson and their saturnine stepdaughter, Katie Slape. Shortly after Philo's arrival, Katie murders Philo's grandfather, leaving Philo to be accused of the crime while the evil trio abscond with the old man's remaining fortune in cash. Through the intervention of a lawyer, Philo escapes back to New Egypt; Katie soon learns of her whereabouts but, missing her, settles for murdering Philo's mother. Hoping to better her lot and to somehow be revenged on Katie and her family, Philo journeys to New York, where much of the novel tells of her gradual rise in the world and the improving fortunes of the Jepsons, who have turned to mass murder for fun and profit with the aid of Katie's second sight. The Jepsons are—unknowingly—directly or indirectly responsible for the death or injury of several of Philo's friends, and Philo—learning of their presence in the city for the first time—vows revenge. As the novel begins to draw to a close she is able to implicate John Jepson as the one responsible for a serious train wreck; he is unceremoniously hanged on the spot by the train crew in a graphically horrible sequence. Hannah Jepson, hiding from New York authorities in Boston, contracts hydrophobia and succumbs to a ghastly death. Katie Slape drops from sight for some time, but is discovered by Philo plying her trade as clairvoyant on a ferryboat; in the ensuing struggle Katie falls overboard as the ferry is docking and is crushed to death between the ferry and the dock, a carpetbag containing the bulk of Philo's grandfather's money dropping from her lifeless hand at Philo's feet.

The epilogue sketches the remaining years of Philo's life as wife, mother and widow, with a final ironic twist involving her fortune that says in essence—despite the earlier series of fortuitous coincidences and tyings-off of loose ends—that "happily ever after" is never as simple or as real as it's supposed to be. As a non-supernatural novel of revenge, *Katie* is the better for the concessions it makes to its "real" world in which revenge can seldom be perfectly achieved. While still a showcase for Michael McDowell's erudition and for his peculiar talent for mayhem and the gruesome, *Katie* also demonstrates a more sophisticated world-view and understanding of the writer's craft than was evident in some of his earlier books. The characters are more fully and more clearly developed; they fit well into their carefully portrayed world and are not simple puppets on the strings of a formulaic plot.

It is interesting to note that *Katie* bears some resemblance to the story of the "Bloody Benders," a family of murderers led by the daughter—named Kate, with pretensions to second sight—who murdered and robbed travelers in Kansas in the early 1870s, and vanished without a trace—as far as history is concerned—when they were detected by the law.

Late 1982 also saw the publication of *Blood Rubies*, a novel of psychological horror involving twins separated at birth, written by McDowell, in collaboration with his close friend Dennis Schuetz, under the pseudonym Axel Young. Under the pseudonym Nathan Aldyne, McDowell and Schuetz have also started a series of detective novels—beginning with *Vermilion* (1982) and *Cobalt* (1982)—concerning the adventures of a gay detective and his straight female companion.

McDowell's most recent solo work debuted in January, 1983, with the publication of *The Flood*, volume I in the mammoth Southern occult novel *Blackwater*. The rest of the novel appeared in five subsequent volumes, *The Levee*, *The House*, *The War*, *The Fortune*, and *Rain* over the next five months. As McDowell has pointed out, such works were not unusual in the 19th century but have so far not been common in modern publishing; the success of historical, science fiction and other genre series novels indicates that it may become a commonplace again.

Though they were published as separate units, the volumes that make up *Blackwater* cannot be read independently of one another. The overall title for the story is somewhat misleading, as was that of *Katie*; the Blackwater River joins with the rusty waters of the Perdido above the small town of Perdido, Alabama, to create the treacherous whirlpool of the Junction that figures largely in the tale, but that river itself has no further significance in the novel beyond the lending of its name. (In reality both rivers do indeed exist, but at no point do they converge; Perdido, Alabama, is a real city, but it and its inhabitants bear no resemblance to the town and characters in *Blackwater*.)

In a sense the volumes of *Blackwater* comprise a lengthy occult soap opera set in the deep South. As the series begins the readers are introduced to the Caskey family, whose members will be the protagonists of the entire novel, and to the mysterious Elinor Dammert, discovered as a major flood begins to recede from Perdido in what had been a completely submerged upper room in Perdido's only hotel. Elinor is both embodiment of most of the horror of *Blackwater* and, in some unexplained way, the catalyst for further horrors to come; for though Oscar Caskey, the man who finds her and eventually marries her, never knows it, Elinor is not human but something monstrous from the depths of the Perdido and the swamps from which it rises, a shapechanger whose real form is that of some slimy, fishlike amphibian creature. The entry of Elinor Dammert into the Caskey family and Perdido life, and the mixing of her strange blood into the Caskey heritage, are the seeds of dark and sweeping changes.

Blackwater spans the years from 1919—on Easter Day, when Elinor is found in the flooded Osceola Hotel in what may be a grotesque comment on the Resurrection—to the spring of 1970, when she dies at the height of a second great flood which, as she had prophesied years before, would wipe Perdido from the face of the earth. In the course of the novel, which details the lives and fortunes of the Caskeys and those around them as well as their gradual rise to positions of enormous influence and wealth, the reader meets other characters like the matriarch Mary-Love, whose machinations against her hated daughter-in-law Elinor have far-reaching consequences but avail her very little, and who dies at the hands of a child Elinor had murdered long before; the servant girl Zaddie Sapp, the black girl who is the first to learn of Elinor's monstrous nature and live to tell of it; John Robert De Bordenave, the retarded child who meets his end in an emotionally wrenching scene as an uncomprehending human sacrifice at Elinor's hands; the gentle and scholarly James Caskey, like Oscar and most of the other male characters more or less a pawn in a unabashedly matriarchal society; Carl Strickland, brutal husband of a Caskey relative, literally broken apart by the unhuman Elinor's avenging strength; Miriam, Elinor's daughter, the indomitable woman who never learns of her inhuman blood, and Frances, her younger sister, who comes to a horrified and uncomprehending knowledge of what she is—and why, and eventually elects to abandon the human world for the muddy. depths of the Perdido—and Nerita, her sister, who has no human characteristics at all.

Blackwater tends to weaken, in terms of its supernatural content, with the third volume, *The War*, and does not regain its occult power until the appearance of the last volume, *Rain*. *Rain* is a sweeping and powerful conclusion to the novel, but nevertheless brings to the book something of what made *The Elementals* unsatisfactory. Old, blind Oscar meets a horrible death at the hands of the undead John Robert, killer of Mary-Love, now accompanied by a baleful simulacrum of the woman he had murdered; there is no real explanation for their appearance. It is almost as if, as in the case of *The Elementals*, they are randomly malevolent forces in quasi-familiar guise, but their very randomness robs them of some of their impact. Elinor, finally showing some signs of her now great age, is accidentally shot by James's illegitimate grandson, a rape-child, as he escapes the clutches of the inhuman Nerita...and as Elinor lies dying, the great rains come again to Perdido. At the moment of her death the murderous spectres of John Robert and Mary-Love vanish as though they had never been; Perdido is once again a ruin, and the monstrous influences from the river—whose influence is so pervasive that the river itself is like an unacknowledged, brooding character for the entirety of the novel, and whose waters, like the sand of *The Elementals*, become a symbol of horror—have apparently withdrawn themselves from the world of men once again.

Blackwater is less than successful for the same reasons *The Elementals* seems less than perfectly successful: the loose ends, the inconsistencies and apparent lapses in logic, remain unfinished and disconnected. The story ending more or less as it began supplies a symmetry which is only partially valid; there are too many inexplicable happenings, too many unanswered—and often unvoiced—questions. Again, this is usually the way real life works; but one of the functions of fiction is to supply a sense of symmetry and continuity, a hope for better things or at least for understanding, that real life so often fails to provide.

There is no question that *Blackwater* is in many ways a considerable achievement; never before has McDowell created as many believable characters, as complex a plot—sustained over great length—or as consistent a use of the malign imagery of natural forces gone to extremes. Like his other novels, *Blackwater* contains scenes of notable horror, but in the end it fails to transcend shorter and more effective novels like *Gilded Needles* in its failure to say anything useful about the human condition.

At present Michael McDowell is one of the biggest names in modern horror fiction, both because he is prolific—and promises to continue to be so—and because, whatever flaws his work might have, he is undeniably one of the most effective writers in the field working today, and has earned high praise from modern masters Peter Straub and Stephen King. As a writer McDowell continues to enjoy, and to rise to, the challenges of new inspiration and of different forms of long fiction; he has attempted some short stories and, while he so far prefers the space the form of the novel provides, he may yet branch out into briefer tales. And, though the change is very gradual indeed, there are signs in McDowell's more recent work that his earlier cynicism might be yielding to a slightly more positive view of humanity, without costing him his touch for either humor or irony and indeed increasing his skill and power with the most shocking and unprecedented images of horror. Michael McDowell is a writer with tales to tell and definite ideas on how to tell them, and I look forward to more of his work; as he continues to write, Michael McDowell continues to fulfill more and more completely the promise of a great talent.

NOTES

I am indebted to Douglas E. Winter's interview with Michael McDowell in *Fantasy Newsletter* (vol. 5, no. 11, December 1982) for the biographical information and personal observations referred to here.

SELECTED BIBLIOGRAPHY

At this writing (November 1983), all of Michael McDowell's books are in print and, with the exception of some volumes of *Blackwater* and *Blood Rubies*, are easily available in larger bookstores.

The Amulet. Avon Books, New York, April 1979. 340 p., $2.50. ISBN 0-380-40584-9.

Cold Moon Over Babylon. Avon Books, New York, February 1980. 292 p., $2.50. ISBN 0-380-48660-1.

Gilded Needles. Avon Books, New York, November 1980. 342 p., $2.50. ISBN 0-380-76398-2.

The Elementals. Avon Books, New York, October 1981. 292 p., $2.95. ISBN 0-380-78360-6.

Katie. Avon Books, New York, September 1982. 295 p., $3.50. ISBN 0-380-80184-1.

Blood Rubies. [with Dennis Scheitz, as 'Axel Young']. Avon Books, New York, 1982. $2.50, ISBN 0-380-79392-x.

Blackwater I: The Flood. Avon Books, New York, January 1983. 189 p., $2.50. ISBN 0-380-81489-7.

Blackwater II: The Levee. Avon Books, New York, February 1983. 191 p., $2.50. ISBN 0-380-82206-7.

Blackwater III: The House. Avon Books, New York, March 1983. 173 p., $2.50. ISBN 0-380-82594-5.

Blackwater IV: The War. Avon Books, New York, April 1983. 187 p., $2.50. ISBN 0-380-82776-x.

Blackwater V: The Fortune. Avon Books, New York, May 1983. 172 p., $2.50. ISBN 0-380-82784-0.

Blackwater VI: Rain. Avon Books, New York, June 1983. 190 p., $2.50. ISBN 0-380-82792-1.

YOURS TRULY, ROBERT BLOCH
By Randall D. Larson

Over the course of nearly fifty years of professional writing, Robert Bloch has dabbled in a great many types of fiction—fantasy, suspense, science fiction, humor, and more; but it is apparent that his most successful forté is that of horror fiction, and he has come to be recognized as a master of the genre. Even in horror, though, Bloch has demonstrated great variety—writing weird fantasies, science fiction horror stories, psychological suspense, even humorous horrors.

Robert Bloch was born in Chicago in 1917, the first child of an urban middle-class family. Although of German-Jewish extraction, the Blochs attended the Methodist Church in Maywood, a Chicago suburb, and the young Bob's religious instruction was learned there. His parents, Raphael A. Bloch, a bank teller, and Stella Loeb Bloch, a school teacher and social worker, gave Bloch an early interest in the performing arts. Early exposure to theatre, and particularly vaudeville, were to influence Bloch's approach to fiction in later years, particularly his distinctive brand of punch-line tales of terror.

When Bloch was ten, his family moved to Milwaukee, Wisconsin, where he became involved in the high school drama department, writing and performing in school vaudeville skits. He began writing short stories in 1932 at the age of 15, selling his first piece two years later. Bloch married Marion Ruth Holcombe in 1940, and took a copywriting position two years later for the Gustav Marx Advertising Agency. A daughter, Sally Ann, was born in 1943. He remained with the advertising agency, writing in his spare time, until 1953 when he moved his family to the small town of Weyauwega, Wisconsin. He stayed there until coming to Hollywood in 1959 to write for television.

Bloch's first marriage ended in divorce in 1963, and he remarried the following year to Eleanor Alexander, recently widowed. Bloch's daughter, Sally Ann, remained with him until she married and moved to northern California. His writing pace slowed but his life was no less hectic with public appearances, film and television assignments and other writing requests, Eleanor and Robert Bloch still live in their home overlooking Topanga Canyon in Los Angeles.

A considerate and gentle person, and a notorious punster, Robert Bloch is the antetype of the cruel villains and fantastic terrors that inhabit his fiction; it remains his insight into human behavior and his cleverness at wordplay that maintains his standing as a master of modern horror fiction.

Bloch's interest in reading horror fiction began with the chance acquisition of a copy of *Weird Tales* in 1927. The stories he read in that issue, combined with the profound effect that Lon Chaney's movies had on him the previous year, began to inspire in Bloch an interest in creative fantasy and horror.

This interest was further compounded when he discovered the work of H.P. Lovecraft, also via *Weird Tales*, and took on a correspondence with the author in 1932. Lovecraft encouraged Bloch to try his own hand at writing weird stories, and two years later Bloch saw the publication of his first tale, "Lilies," in William Crawford's semi-professional magazine, *Marvel Tales*. By the end of 1934, Bloch had sold several stories to the very magazine that sparked his interest, *Weird Tales*.

The first of them appeared in the January 1935 issue. "The Feast in the Abbey," while actually being the second story Bloch sold to the magazine, had the good fortune of appearing first, and it was a strong debut for the young writer, much more so than his first sale which appeared later: "The Secret of the Tomb," a mild fantasy of a man who discovers his ancestor is a ghoul.

"The Feast in the Abbey" remains a pleasant horror story, and its last line—as Bloch's carefully contrived endings are known for—still has a powerful bite. Bloch carefully sets the stage for his ultimate revelation—that the main course of a lavish feast served the narrator by a group of unusual monks in a hidden Monastery, is in actuality the corpse of the narrator's lost brother—and Bloch springs it at the very end, leaving the reader hanging alone to deal with that grisly revelation.

This style—that of building to a certain point and then flinging a horrific shock upon the reader—was a familiar one in the pages of *Weird Tales* and particularly in the work of Lovecraft—a natural enough model for the young Bloch to emulate. But whereas Lovecraft's shock endings generally were in the form of horrifying realization—the awesome confirmation of what the narrator has suspected all along—Bloch tended to prefer hitherto-unexpected surprises, carefully supported by the preceding storyline but rarely anticipated in advance. As Bloch developed as a writer, these punch-line endings (frequently mixing humor and horror, in the form of a sordid pun) became his trademark, and few writers accomplished it as effectively as Bloch. Most of Bloch's early horror tales were conceived and executed in this fashion, emulating the Lovecraft style in both structure and language, with wordy, formal narration, adjective-rich description, capped by the ultimate revelation.

Bloch received permission to use Lovecraft himself as a character in "The Shambler from the Stars" (1935), his fourth published story, and Bloch even killed off his elder mentor in ghoulish fashion. (Lovecraft returned the favor a year later in his own "The Haunter of the Dark" and Bloch responded to conclude the trilogy in "The Shadow From the Steeple," 1950.) "Shambler" is also ripe with many in-jokes known mostly to Bloch and fellow-members of the "Lovecraft circle," who shared friendship and fictional ideals with Lovecraft. Just as Lovecraft would often incorporate a collegue's's name into one of his stories (such as Klarkash-ton, for Clark Ashton Smith, in "The Whisper in Darkness"), Bloch too enjoyed such private amusement in these early tales, spurred by the camaraderie of the Lovecraft circle.

During this period Bloch also took an interest in Egyptian mythology, using the milieu in several weird stories, most of which have something to do with the fulfillment of an ancient Egyptian curse. "The Opener of the Way" (1936), "The Secret of Sebek" (1937), "Fane of the Black Pharoah" (1937) and "Beetles" (1938), all dealt with diabolical Egyptology, in some cases correlating Lovecraft's fictional Cthulhu Mythos canon with the Egyptian milieu. Other memorable tales of the '30s include "Waxworks" (1939), a macabre tale of ritualistic murder propagated through the sorcerous wax figure of a long-dead witch; and "The Cloak" (1939) a fine story about the influence of a vampire's cloak upon its Halloween wearer, and a tale which in narrative and plot shows Bloch's beginning to move away from the Lovecraft idiom.

Many of these early stories are simple exercises in shock-endings, though, with little substance in theme or character. They exist simply for the pleasure of springing their ghoulish climaxes upon the reader—like macabre jokes. While this form of entertainment remains Bloch's staple, his work began to grow into *more* than simple sordid gags through the consistent themes that he chose to express. It wasn't too long after Lovecraft's death in 1937 that Bloch began to explore his own interests in narrative style and story concept, and this led him into his own distinctive niche—that of the psychological thriller.

The horrors of his Lovecraftian period were primarily supernatural dangers; grand, cosmic malevolences preying upon an insignificant mankind; Bloch gradually became more interested in human horror, the kind he read about every day in the newspaper and heard nightly on the radio. And so, it was not so much the external horrors that were to figure henceforth in his stories, those fanciful terrors out of mythology and imagination that—when the story was finished and the magazine put aside—often ceased to be real; but it was the *internal* terrors, the ugly, twisted recesses of the human mind and the awful deeds it could inspire that would motivate his stories—and they created a far more intense brand of horror because they were recognized as being real—they struck a chord in the readers.

This new vein, of course, had its most prominent effect on his nonfantasy crime and suspense novels, though in fact it can be found even in some of his earliest science fiction and fantasy tales, whether simply through the use of psychological attitudes spoken by a character (as in "The Dark Demon," 1936), the use of a psychologist *as* a character (the narrator in "The Grinning Ghoul," 1936), or more importantly through the exploration of the psychological aspects of his characters through the narrative (as in "Slave of the Flames," 1938, and his pivotal science fiction story of the same year, "The Strange Flight of Richard Clayton").

Bloch's famous and oft-reprinted story of 1943, "Yours Truly, Jack the Ripper," delves into three psychological aspects and is given a different style of writing, characterized by fast-moving narrative sentences and dialog, culminating in one of the best horrific punch lines Bloch has ever written. The story mingles the terror of the known—that of the infamous Ripper murders of Victorian England—with the supernatural fantasy of *Weird Tales*—the murders are actually sacrificial rituals to grant the Ripper eternal life.

Like the distinctively structured horror-fantasies for earlier *Weird Tales*, "Yours Truly, Jack the Ripper" gradually builds toward a shocking climax which will put all that has gone before into a new context and achieve its horror not only through the shock of revelation but through the implication of what that revelation means. In this story, it's that Jack the Ripper is not safely hidden away in the historical past of Victorian London, but that in essence he exists among us all. Today. It's the awareness of the violence in our world that makes the terror of "Yours Truly, Jack the Ripper" so intense.

Bloch's awareness of this fact shaped all of his fiction from this point on. Although he did not completely abandon the fantastic beings and places of early works, he began to approach them from this new perspective. "The Skull of the Marquis de Sade" (1945), like the Ripper story, transformed an infamous figure from history into a supernatural malevolency, lending its protagonist a similarly violent end. "Enoch" (1946) was a frightening story of a psychotic murderer whose terrible deeds are commanded by an unseen demon who may—or may not—actually exist. "Lizzie Borden Took an Axe" (1946) dealt with another historical murderer whose crimes, spurred by supernatural powers, reach through the years to influence contemporary protagonists. "The Cheaters" (1947) tells of a set of spectacles with sorcerous powers that causes it wearers to see *inwardly*, into people's true nature, rather than outwardly, and the subconscious terrors they see doom them to self-destruction. In "The Man Who Collected Poe" (1951), the obsessive aberrations of a particularly fervent collector manages to reanimate the very corpse of the famed writer. "Lucy Comes to Stay" (1952), a forerunner of Bloch's famous 1959 novel, *Psycho*, describes a young woman driven to murder, as in "Enoch," by a friendly companion who in this case is revealed to be a separate personality of the woman herself. "The Real Bad Friend" (1957) was an even stronger presentation of the same theme.

As Bloch ventured into these new areas of horror, his style developed as well. He abandoned the Lovecraftian narration of his earlier work and took on a style characterized by fast-moving sentence structure and often tongue-in-cheek use of puns and plays-on-words. "The House of the Hatchet" (1941) is an early example; the first-person narrative fairly breezes along as its cynical narrator visits a haunted house and becomes influenced by the murdering spirit of its former inhabitant. The narrative style not only brings the characters to life—both the narrator (whose attitudes and perspective colors the narrative) and the other characters we see through his observations—but makes the story remarkably readable. This is a characteristic of much of Bloch's work—the manner in which he *tells* his stories is often just as entertaining as the stories themselves. "Black Bargain" (1942) is another example of Bloch's use of this narrative style, especially in the vivid descriptions of the customers who patronize the narrator's tavern. Above all, Bloch is a perceptive observer of humankind, and his unique observations add to the lifelike reality of the characters who people these stories.

Bloch's horror fiction also became distinctive for its restraint, in terms of graphic violence. While many of his early Lovecraftian stories described their terrors in ludicrous detail, his work subsequent to the '30s avoided this description completely. The gruesome murders that figured so prominently in "Yours Truly, Jack the Ripper," "Lizzie Borden Took an Axe," "The House of the Hatchet" and others are never described outright. Rather, Bloch takes the occasion to shock us with a sudden punch-line, usually at the end of the story or chapter, and often veiled in tongue-in-cheek wordplay, as in the brilliant puns that conclude "Catnip" (1948), "I Like Blondes" (1956), "The Deadliest Art" (1958), and "The Night Before Christmas" (1980), both amusing us in narrative irony as well as horrifying us in its plot implications. It's this restraint in story-telling which sets Bloch aside from many other horror writers, particularly in the current vogue of graphic violence and "splatter" horror in both films and literature.

Other stories of the '40s continued this trend. "Sweets to the Sweet" (1947) is a not-so-sweet story of a mistreated little girl who exacts a painful vengeance on her cruel father through the use of a lifelike doll. "Catnip" (1948) deals with a recurring theme in Bloch's fiction, that of murder and justice. A rotten kid terrorizes an old woman who happens to be a witch, eventually killing her when one of his pranks goes awry. The witch's cat makes amends however, and the story ends with memorable punch-line. "The Sorcerer's Apprentice" (1949) is an effective psychological portrait of its protagonist, a down-on-his-luck drifter who becomes an assistant to a carnival magician. He soon becomes the pawn of the magician's wife in a plot to kill her husband, but inadvertently avenges him by attempting to emulate the magician's act—and winds up sawing the wife in two.

Much of Bloch's work during the '50s consisted of nonfantasy work for mystery and detective magazines, as well as not-infrequent excursion into comic farce, such as the Lefty Feep stories he had been writing for *Fantastic Adventures* since the early '40s. He also began to write nonfiction for some of the higher-paying men's magazines, but he didn't neglect horror altogether, and his horror fiction of this decade remains among his best work.

A return to the Lovecraftian idiom with "The Shadow from the Steeple" (1950), Bloch's followup to HPL's "The Haunter of the Dark," demonstrated his contemporary approach to the type of horror fiction he started out in, as his novel, *Strange Eons*, did even more so thirty years later. While the majority of "Shadow's" narrative is written in a Lovecraftian style, related through verbose flashback, the opening and closing scenes are depicted via Bloch's own fast-moving and slightly playful narrative voice.

Bloch followed "Shadow" with another Cthulhu Mythos story the following year, "Notebook Found in a Deserted House" (1951), which was given an effective touch through its being told by a 12-year-old boy, whose language and perception enlivens the narration.

In 1953 Bloch was given the opportunity to collaborate, posthumously, with Edgar Allan Poe when he was asked to complete Poe's unfinished story, "The Lighthouse." For this moody tale of isolation and the willing-forth of a companion out of the sea to slack the narrator's solitude, Bloch studied Poe's writing in order to adopt the style of his elder collaborator and to culminate the story in a manner suitable to Poe's apparent intentions.

"The Hungry House" (1950) is Bloch's handling of the haunted house theme, concerning the posthumous influence of a vain old woman whose spirit exists in the reflective surfaces of mirrors or glasspanes, and drives others to imitate her suicide. "Mr. Steinway" (1954) tells of a piano whose unusual fellowship with its mystic-minded pianist brings it to malevolent life, resulting in jealousy and murder. "I Kiss Your Shadow" (1956) is a ghost story concerning love and lust that extends beyond the grave.

"You Could Be Wrong" (1955) is a frightening tale of paranoia—Harry Jessup gets so wound up by phoneyness and fakery in the media, in fashion, in government, that he soon suspects that the whole country is one big imitation, maintained by aliens who destroyed the original—the ravings of any average paranoid delusion, until the story ends on a particularly chilling note. "I Like Blondes" (1956), Bloch's first sale to *Playboy*, told of a peculiar womanizer with an obsession with fair-haired young lovelies, for reasons made plain in the beautifully-set-up final line. "Broomstick Ride" (1957) examines the conflict between science and superstition as explorers from Earth confront the natives on a planet ruled by witchcraft, and pay warmly for their disbelief.

"Man With a Hobby" (1957) is a particularly effective story of a mass-murderer, not a psychological examination as in "Enoch," but a straight gimmick-story with a clever and surprising ending line—the story does contain an interesting commentary on violence as the narrator and the suspected murderer converse in a bar in the midst of a bowler's convention. "Sweet Sixteen" (1958) is a dark horror story of satanism and demonic sacrifice, telling of a town whose teenagers have literally "sold out" to the devil, willingly overcome with demonic possession. The story is Bloch's commentary on youth violence, taken a few steps further and coupled with demonic horror. "Hungarian Rhapsody" (1958) deals with an attempted murderer thwarted by the victim, who just happens to be a vampire and exacts a sharp justice upon the criminal. "Sleeping Beauty" (1958) concerns a man, returning to visit New Orleans, who accepts an invitation to patronize one of the last parlour houses, only to be robbed in a scam that reaches across time—the elegant hooker he'd spent the night with is found, when he returns with the police to retrieve his stolen wallet, to be a rotting skeleton...

"The Pin" (1954) is a notable horror story telling of a little fat man who lives in a condemned office building and sticks his pin into random phone books and makes people die, discovered by the protagonist who is fated to take his place and maintain the tradition of—death. It's both a quirky and pointedly frightening look at the aimlessness of death, over which man has no control; the inevitability of dying, of disease, of unwanted tragedy. Once again, Bloch finds the horrors of real life, exaggerated as they are in "The Pin," far more frightening than the supernatural monstrosities of earlier days, and he continues to explore them—exorcising those fears, as it were, via the typewriter—in his horror fiction.

In spite of his prolific output, the '50s was a bitter period for Bloch, personally. He nourished a growing pessimism toward what he felt was an endless treadmill upon which he had to write and write and *write* without satisfaction, just in order to make ends meet. His personal depression resulted in an increasingly pessimistic tone in many of his stories.

In particular his psychological novels dealt with the gritty, unpleasant world of psychopathic violence peopled with evil persons who otherwise as average as anyone you'd expect to meet walking down the street. Bloch's growing interest in practical psychology and his remarkable ability to create a villain in chilling psychological detail—putting the reader in his shoes through a disturbing first-person narrative yet retaining the moral quality of right and wrong that refuses to condone the villain's activities or point of view—these were to characterize his distinctive brand of horror fiction throughout the '50s.

During the last few years of the decade, though, embittered with despondency, Bloch poured his disillusionment into his short fiction. "Daybroke" (1958) is a grim, bitterly pessimistic story of future war, as seen through the eyes of a survivor who wanders through the wasted ruins of nuclear destruction. Eventually he winds up in a military building, speaking with a weary general as they survey the wreckage. "To think of our being beaten," the protagonist moans. "What do you mean, man?" the general replies, proudly—"We won!". This is Bloch's dismal comment to those inclined toward scorekeeping in the face of a no-win situation. "Report on Sol III" (1958) is a dismal view, shrouded in mild parody, of the human condition as seen through the eyes of alien explorers who decide there's nothing of value to be had on Earth. Even Bloch's Hugo-winning fantasy, "That Hell-Bound Train" (1958), mirrored Bloch's cynicism as it explored the unease of a man, trying to thwart a deal with the devil, who continually seeks the right moment of satisfaction at which to stop time, but in his greedy search for a "better high" fails to find it until the ironically hellish conclusion.

"Funnel of God" (1959) is Bloch's bleak metaphor for the human condition as he was then perceiving it, describing in quasi-allegorical terms a young boy's fascination with a childhood bogeyman who haunts him throughout his life. While thinly veiled as a horror story on the bogeyman theme, "Funnel of God" was Bloch's most philosophical story of the period, and an extraordinarily depressing tale of existential bleakness, devoid of hope or satisfaction.

1960, however, found Bloch in much better spirits, and once again the sense of optimism and frivolity returned to his work. *Psycho* was being made into a motion picture, Bloch had begun writing for television and moved his family to Hollywood. He'd side-stepped the endless treadmill and found new energy and satisfaction in what he was doing, and his work reflected this brighter outlook.

Even while becoming involved in Hollywood screenwriting (with mixed luck, though: most of his scriptwork wound up being altered by producers or TV executives who fancy themselves better experts in horror than Bloch—and most of it, adaptations for *Dark Room*, TV-movies like *The Cat Creature* and *The Dead Don't Die*, has suffered from such heavy-handed "improvement"; Bloch's best screenwriting work remains his adaptations for *Thriller*, *Alfred Hitchcock Presents* and his Amicus Films trilogy), he has continued to be active in the literary field.

His becoming involved with the movies might have seemed inevitable, and was certainly a welcome opportunity for him, having nurtured a love for movies all his life. Hollywood, in fact, was a theme frequently recurring in his horror stories even in the '40s, expressing both his love for the art of movies and moviemaking (not to mention his encyclopedic knowledge of the silent movie era), and his cynicism toward the cut-throat business practices that remain in control of the art form. At the same time, Hollywood's collective cast of characters, both before and behind the scenes, fueled Bloch's penchant for examining varied personalities, and his perceptive observations of crowds and individuals in his work is revealing and fascinating—often disturbing.

"The Dream-Makers" (1953) is Bloch's tribute to the silent movie era, telling of a writer who discovers that the silent film stars all faded out of the business when the talkies came in because they had been written out of life's *script* by omniscient Fates, who control the flow of history in the manner of a movie script—if certain individuals fail to follow this script they are (literally) cut out.

"Terror Over Hollywood" (1957) explains the truth behind the long careers of Hollywood stars—a selected few are turned into automatons through an extensive operation, their brains transferred into synthetic bodies in order to live longer, sacrificing human pleasures for enduring Fame and Stardom. "Talent" (1960) is about an unusual boy with an uncanny ability to impersonate the movie characters he loves—with disastrous consequences for the city of Los Angeles. "The Plot is the Thing" (1966) told of a brain operation meant to cure a woman's obsessive retreat from reality into old horror films, but which transfers her into a bizarre movie-world in she finds herself dissolving from scene to scene, terrorized by monster after monster. "The Movie People" (1969) proferred the idea that movie extras, after death, continue to live on in old movie scenes—whether or not they actually appeared in the movie in question. They turn up, discretely, in the midst of large crowd scenes, to watch the people in the audience..

The '60s also saw Bloch's return to a theme he first touched in the '40s—Jack the Ripper. "A Toy for Juliette" (1967) was written at Harlan Ellison's request for his *Dangerous Visions* anthology. In this powerful futuristic horror tale, Juliette is a sadistic nymphomaniac who is given human "gifts" by her grandfather, plucked from various moments in history in his time machine; she makes use of the toys for perverse pleasure, killing them at the moment of ecstasy. She finds grandfather's latest "toy" much to her liking, but when she reaches for her knife to finish him off, she receives a pointed lesson in justice from the Victorian gentleman that grandfather plucked from foggy London . . . . Jack returned in "A Most Unusual Murder" (1976), in which a student of the Ripper murders locates the original medical bag belonging to the Ripper (or so he thinks), only to end up mimicking his crimes in a scuffle with the time-traveling collector who originally found it. Bloch's interest in the Ripper (and other historical murderers which have figures in his work, as in his 1974 novelization of the H.H. Holmes crimes, *American Gothic*) peaked in his latest novel-length treatment, *Night of the Ripper* (1984).

Much of Bloch's horror fiction of the '70s and '80s dealt with themes that figured greatly in his crime and suspense fiction of the '50s: murder and justice—usually an especially poetic justice for the murderer. "The Double Whammy" (1970) takes place in a carnival, telling of a behind-the-scenes romance that results in suicide when the girl is spurned, and the foul revenge of the girl's mother, the carnival's fortune teller. "Funny Farm" (1971) concerns the robbery of an old comic collector by a young thief who desires the valuable books but winds up killing the owner in rage when he discovers the old man collected "worthless" comic *strips*—not books. The thief is further enraged when he is uncomically done in by living representations of the old man's collection. "The Animal Fair" (1971) dealt with murder and justice more obliquely. It's described primarily in the form of flashbacks, told to the protagonist by the owner of Captain Ryder's gorilla show. Years ago, Ryder's daughter was raped and killed by crazed Hollywood hippies, sending him into a fruitless search for vengeance. He interrupts his story to talk of his animal show, remarking about legends of African witchdoctors who were said to sew up drugged victims in animal skins and train them in savagery until the unfortunate native literally *became* the animal. The protagonist is puzzled by the strange story until he recalls Ryder's threat of vengeance against the hippie leader, and culminates with his brutal realization of the true nature of Ryder's gorilla companion. A remarkable work of subtlety and terror-by-implication, the story is also Bloch's commentary on the violence of Charles Manson-type counterculture groups, as dramatized by the hippie gang in the story.

Another excellent story of subtle terror is "Nina" (1977), which describes a torrid affair between Nolan, an American contractor working in South America, and Nina, the mysterious native girl who appears to visit him night after night. A villagewoman named Mama Dolores warns him to beware of her because she's one of the snake people—ancient hybrids who become human to mate with men. Nolan scoffs, of course, but when his wife and infant son come to join him, he spurns Nina and kicks her out. The mysterious native girl is livid with rage, but takes her leave. The next morning Nolan wakes to find Mama Dolores dead and his small son missing—he asks about Nina, is told she's left. Nolan suspects she kidnapped his son, but a native worker tells him she left emptyhanded—but the worker's subsequent remark puts Nina's departure and her attributes in an entirely new light, and leaves the reader awash in a cold sweat. The final line is so subtle one almost has to read it twice to get it—and that paradoxically adds to its power.

"What You See Is What You Get" (1977) involves a camera that takes pictures predicting when and how the subject will die; the pro-tagonist puts it to good use, ultimately committing a murder himself when he misinterprets the photo showing his own demise. "The Freak

Show" (1979) is an intriguing examination of human violence and apathy, as represented by a group of townsfolk invited to a traveling carnival who wind up *becoming* the main exhibit, an unusual and sordid form of Blochesque justice—this time in penance for attitudes more so than actual deeds. It's Bloch the moralist again, suggesting that what's beneath the surface is often just as deadly as what is seen above.

"The Night Before Christmas" (1980) deals with an adulterous affair between an artist and the wife of the wealthy businessman hired to paint her portrait. The affair is discovered by the husband, who perpetrates a grisly vengeance, revealed with another of Bloch's best punch-line endings, this one both subtle and graphic at the same time.

Bloch continued to mix humor with his horror stories, not only in the form of pun-endings as in "The Night Before Christmas," but in more zany works such as the hysterical "A Case of the Stubborns" (1976), in which a backwoods grandfather dies but fails to recognize the fact until his young grandson bugs him with an appropriate solution to make the fact plain. "The Closer of the Way" (1977) is an effective bit of self-parody in which Bloch himself is committed to an asylum and suspected insane due to his bizarre stories with their themes of murder, insanity, demon possession, decapitation. Bloch satirizes himself while at the same time examining on his own the themes that have recurred in his fiction and obliquely responding to those who accuse horror writers of all being sick—and concludes the tale with an effective recapitulation of "The Feast in the Abbey."

"Picture" (1979) is a humorous Deal-with-the-Devil story (the Deceiver, this time, appearing in the reasonable guise of a Beverly Hills psychiatrist), in which the protagonist sells his soul for one night of pleasure with the girl of his dreams, only to be bilked when the deal comes up short. The story is structured like similar Devil-dealing stories that Bloch has written, but in this case the narrative is purely satirical, Satan described as a witty, literally devil-may-care humorist.

While on the surface level, Bloch is primarily telling an entertaining story, it becomes apparent that, taken as a whole, Bloch's horror fiction (as with his other types of fiction) nonetheless is a mode of communication for a writer who has something to say about the world we live in. Behind the often-frolicsome narration, behind the carefully crafted psychological character portraits, behind the skillfully launched punch-lines: lies exposed Bloch the man. Bloch the human being, with the convictions and concerns infused from a lifetime of observing others. In the final analysis, what Bloch is writing is nearly always a morality piece. Not only in his frequent explorations of themes of good and evil, but in the underlying depth of thought that lies behind the horrors and fantasies of his fiction.

CONCERNING DAVID CASE
By Jeffrey Goddin

I am sometimes a fan of contemporary horror fiction, but I've often felt that if one wants to find the *masters* of 20th century horror, one must go back to such writers as Lovecraft, Machen, Blackwood, or E.L. White. I do, however, have an exception to this possibly rash judgment: David Case.

David Francis Case is an American writer whose output—in the horror genre—has been slim. His major horror works consist of a recent novel somewhat in the mode of Sax Rohmer, *The Third Grave* (Arkham House, 1981), a chilling Gothic called *Fengriffen* (Hill and Wang, 1970), and, earliest of the three, a collection of three novellas, *The Cell: Three Tales of Horror* (Hill and Wang, 1969). *The Third Grave* is entertaining, but it is with the latter two books that Case's reputation justly rests.

Fengriffen is a gothic tale to the bone. There is an old mansion, Fengriffen House, a brooding Lord, a beautiful young bride, a sinister legend and an even more sinister woodsman. There have been superficially similar tales for a couple of centuries, yet, by his narrative skill and powers of description, Case manages to set this tale above the rest.

The story proceeds with the inevitability of Poe—indeed, there is something of Roderick Usher in the character of Charles Fengriffen, and of his grim ancestor, a man of demonic drive and demonic desires. As in the manner of older tales of the genre, the protagonist and narrator is a doctor—Pope, a psychologist—come to try and aid the beautiful bride, Catherine.

Like others of Case's characters, Pope is both involved and self-aware, and it is partially this self-awareness that makes him such a fine narrative figure:

> I donned a heavy cape of Scottish wool and changed my light stick for a heavy cudgel I had procured in the Swiss Alps. As my hand closed upon the thick shaft, I felt a touch of irony in the fact that a man of science should take heart and comfort from a length of carved hardwood. Yet such is man, and to say that a man

knows himself is to say that he has looked into a bottomless chasm and claimed discovery...(p. 47)

The image of the chasm is apt, for Pope, the man of science, is drawn as inexorably as helpless Catherine into a realization of the final horror.

This tale, by the way, is a precursor of a number of abominable tales and movies, such as *The Entity*, with incubi/succubi themes. But Case's handling is vastly more subtle, rather in the manner of Poe, or Le Fanu.

Fengriffen is a fine tale, though somewhat predictable. The latter is not true of the novellas in *The Cell*. These tales are unique, and it is these stories, specifically "The Dead End" and "The Hunter," that show Case at his best.

"The Dead End" is a synthesis of two sub-genres of fantastic literature: that which includes the exploration of an exotic place with strange consequences—"Weird Adventure," if you will—and that of the mad scientist. Both sub-genres are brought totally and believably into a contemporary mode by Case's masterful narration.

The protagonist, an ambitious young anthropologist, is sent to a remote region of Tierra del Fuego to investigate the appearance of a mysterious creature, somewhat akin to the "yeti" in habit, which hints of a "missing link."

Although not without its resident Englishman (there must, to judge from the literature, be an eccentric Englishman living in every obscure corner of the globe, sipping gin 'n tonics at noon), the Tierra del Fuego that Case depicts has a fine air of "alienness" suitable to weird adventure:

Night was deepening the sky beneath the darkened clouds when I found myself at the end of the modern world—the outskirts of Ushuaia. I had a very concrete sense of standing at a barrier. Behind me electric and neon blanketed the town, which civilization had penetrated, although it lay in a thin veneer within the boundaries, its roots shallow and precarious, a transplant that had not yet taken a firm hold. Before me the land broke upwards and away, jagged and barren and dotted with clusters of sheet metal shacks painted in the brightest tones, oranges and yellows and reds. The thin chimneys rattled bravely in the wind, and the smoke lay in thin, flat ribbons. Kerosene lamps cast futile pastel light in the doorways, and a few shrouded figures moved. (p. 167)

From this point of "civilization" the protagonist must penetrate the wilds, guided by a gigantesque, mute Indian to search out an eccentric scientist living in a adjacent region to that of the "missing link." Here Case's superb narrative skill, his ability to "trap" the reader in his protagonist's world, comes especially to the fore:

> The land had changed once more on the far bank of the stream. We were traversing dense forests. The rocks and boulders were still there on all sides, but they were hidden and engulfed by the trees and shrubbery. The undergrowth was heavy, and I couldn't see the horse's legs beneath the knees, yet he carried on steadily enough on this invisible ground. Moss braided my shoulders and clung around my neck like Hawaiian leis. It was cooler here, the sun blocked out and earth damp. I put my windbreaker on again. We passed through an open space and back into the shade, through patterns of light and shadow, moving chiaroscuro imprinted on the senses. I was still sweating, but the moisture was cold, and I was aware of my discontent now, the blunted sensations of the hot afternoon sharpened unpleasantly. I became conscious of time again, hoping we had not far to go, and looked at my watch. It surprised me to find it was seven o'clock. We had been riding virtually without pause for ten hours. The Indian seemed as fresh as he had when we started, and who knew how long he'd ridden to reach Ushuaia that morning. It seemed impossible that anyone, even that extraordinary man, could have travelled through this terrain through the night, and yet we pushed on with no sign of a halt. (p. 195)

Shortly after this point the focus of the tale begins to shift subtly from the search for the dangerous "missing link" to the realm of the renegade scientist, a man who has a fine, contemporary knowledge of genetics, but who, in his study of human evolution, has preferred to live in such an isolated area as the mountains of Tierra del Fuego for twenty years. The extent of the scientist's eccentricity begins to make an impression on the reader, and an experienced reader of weird fiction will begin to have "suspicions" regarding the relationship of this scientist with the "missing link." But Case succeeds in coming up with a much more horrible ending than simple "missing-link-eats-man." The horror of the climax is almost metaphysical in implication, and relates to one of the most vulnerable areas of human emotion: sexuality.

As fine a tale as is "The Dead End," it is totally eclipsed by "The Hunter." "The Hunter" is a story not only of the protagonist's quest to discover the source of some especially gruesome murders on the moors of Dartmoor, but also a story of self-awareness. In his search for the creature, he finds he must become reconciled with a subtle element of himself—an element of the primitive, but blended with human values—which emerges during his quest. It is also a tale, almost philosophically, about the nature of fear.

Wetherby, once a highly skilled hunter and stalker, is brought out of a quiet, British-club sort of retirement to help investigate a series of gruesome slayings. The murders are as weird as they are horrible, for they hint of an animal of supernatural powers, not unlike a werewolf would possess, if such a thing could be.

Wetherby is stumped, and through his inability to find—or even identify—the weird killer, and the tension of his nocturnal stalks, begins to question his ability to fill this role—which, in spite of himself, has become crucially important to him. A pivotal scene is one which, revealing Case's descriptive powers at their best, we, and Wetherby, realize that he has made a potentially fatal error:

> Wetherby came to the top of the ridge beside a mound of rocks and stood there, looking down. The stream wound through the moonlight like the slimy track of a snail and the open land between was silver filigreed by the slender shadows of the reeds. Wetherby stood very still and looked. If anything was moving down there, he would have seen its shadow beneath it. This was the first night that the moon had been his ally. But nothing moved, and he saw little sense in proceeding farther in that direction. He decided he would follow the crest of the ridge back to the secondary road, carefully circling each rocky mound...
>
> Wetherby jumped with the realization.
>
> For a moment he quivered, taut and tight, and then he relaxed, cursing his stupidity. He had made his first blunder. He had climbed the ridge and stood beside that high peak of stone, hardly noticing it. He had stood there for several minutes. If the killer had been lurking in those rocks, Wetherby would have died beside them. It was unbelievable carelessness, a mistake he would never have made in the past, a routine that had been second nature to him—until now. (pp. 142-143)

Wetherby's character is balanced against that of Byron, his former hunting mate, who still leads the life of adventure that

Wetherby has foresaken. But Byron, out of disdain for the needs of the few unadventurous humans whom the unknown beast slays, refuses to aid in the hunt, indeed, philosophically sides with the slayer. A tense dichtomy develops between the philosophies of the two men, against the backdrop of more gruesome slayings and their effects on the rural populace.

For the effect of these events is to create in the citizens of the area of rural Dartmoor the greatest fear that they've ever known:

> It was a blanket of fear, invisible but oppressive and intense, and it covered the moors like an overcast sky, more ominous than an impending storm. The fear was all the greater because the people did not know what it was they feared, what the monstrous being was that had three times struck so terribly. They no longer spoke of it often, as they had at first, for the fear had increased with each killing, and reached absolute intensity with the death of Hazel Lake, peacefully reading by her fireside. This was a people who had long regarded their home as their castle, sanctuary inviolate, and a new dimension was added to their terror. Nowhere was safe, this fiend might come at any time, to any place, and anyone might be his next victim. It wasn't death itself that brought such consuming fear, it was the unknown quality of their death, the method of dying and the agony of wondering if the creature would strike again...where it would strike...whom it would kill. Superstition, never far below the surface of civilized minds, came bubbling up in globules of terror, bursting and enflaming the brain. (p. 130)

Wetherby, as he stalks the moors by night to try and lure the killer from cover, is forced into an interior quest which matches his exterior hunt, until, finally, he slips into a kind of primitive awareness that enables him to find a clear path, both to the killer, and to his own psyche.

The theme is not unique, but with skillful shifts of perspective, incisive characterization, taunt evocations of atmosphere, and even the occasional interjection of humor to vary the pace, Case weaves a compelling narrative of this very special hunt, and of the hunter.

I have seen David Case compared to Algernon Blackwood. I have read all of Blackwood's published short fiction—which fills a row of volumes in my library—and I can find little basis for this comparison. True, Blackwood wrote a few tales involving Egyptian magic, as does Case in *The Third Grave*. And true, Blackwood often set his tales either in the "moors" or the "shires"—or locales that would be more exotic to his readers, as does Case; and true, both are masters of the extended narrative descriptive passage.

But a basic difference between the two is that Blackwood was concerned above all with the mythical, elemental forces of nature, their reflection within us and sometimes their menace to man. Case is no pantheist. His horrors, even his supernatural ones, have their root in the horrors of the twisted human psyche.

Someone to whom Case *does* bear a strong resemblance, especially in this treatment of fear and self-preservation as themes, is the suspense master, Geoffrey Household (*Rogue Male, A Rough Shoot, Watcher in the Shadows*). The awareness of primitive senses, particularly of the stalking sense, which his protagonists sometimes reach, is quite similar to that of Household's protagonists. His work also bears some resemblance, in a tale such as "The Dead End," to some of Conan Doyle's non-Holmesian weird fiction, such as "When the World Screamed," in his use of the motif of the young expert meeting with the old, eccentric master—but then, many have used this motif. Blackwood? Can't see it.

David Case is a skilled narrator, and has a particular talent for extrapolating established sub-genres such as the Hunt, the Weird Adventure, the Mad Scientist, the Werewolf, Incubi and Succubi, and others, into a setting thoroughly and believably modern. His special talent lies in his ability to detach this setting, by its very realism, and thus the experiences of his protagonist, from a world that is comfortable and safe. The protagonist is thoroughly trapped, to quote Coleridge, by a "willful suspension of disbelief"—and the reader with him.

BIBLIOGRAPHY

The Cell, and Other Tales of Horror. London: Macdonald, 1969. Includes "The Cell," "The Hunter," "The Dead End."

The Cell: Three Tales of Horror. New York: Hill & Wang, 1970. Includes "The Cell," "The Hunter," "The Dead End."

Fengriffen: A Chilling Tale. New York: Hill & Wang, 1970.

Fengriffen and Other Stories. London: Macdonald, 1971.

Fengriffen. New York: Lancer, date unknown.

(Fengriffen). And Now the Screaming Starts. London: Pan, 1973.

The Third Grave. Sauk City, WI: Arkham House, 1981.

Wolf Tracks. New York: Tower Books, 1980.

THE SUBTLE TERRORS OF CHARLES L. GRANT
by Don D'Ammassa

Charles L. Grant has during the past decade established himself firmly as one of the leading novelists, short story writers, and editors in the field of horror fiction. Born in 1942, Grant attended Trinity College majoring in history, and subsequently entered the teaching profession. Shortly after making his first professional sale, a short story, Grant was drafted and found himself serving as a military policeman in Vietnam, which effectively stalled his career as a writer until the early 1970s.

Although initially typed as a science fiction author (in which field he has produced a small but interesting body of work as well), Grant showed an early interest in what has come to be known as "Dark Fantasy" and horror fiction. His dissatisfaction with certain aspects of teaching culminated in his departure from that field and his current fulltime status as a writer and editor. His ongoing series of original anthologies of short supernatural fiction, *Shadows*, reflects his personal philosophies about what a good horror story should be.

Grant insists that there is a difference between shock and horror. The recent flurry of films about mass murderers, replete with gory details, may evoke feelings of revulsion, but does not employ what Grant sees as the subtler effects of true horror. Eschewing for the most part traditional monsters such as vampires and werewolves, he is more interested in making his reader increasingly uneasy about reality, hopefully culminating in a frightening uncertainty that will linger even after the last page has been turned. In his introduction to *Shadows 6*, he states explicitly: "And that is perhaps the single greatest fear that any of us ever have—that what we know to be true, that what we know is so and will not change because it has never changed before, isn't true anymore, isn't so, and everything can change, not always for the better."

In an article for the fan magazine, *Knights*, Grant discussed the criteria for a good horror story. Characters must be well drawn enough that the reader cares about their ultimate fate. There must be a successful creation of mood along with a solid plot framework. There must be suspense created in terms of the ultimate outcome of the story. No matter what we might suspect will happen, no matter how certain we might be that we know how things will ultimately turn out, there must still be some element of doubt that controls our attention until the final scene. Recognizing that most readers really don't believe in the supernatural, he accepts that this makes successful horror fiction that much more difficult to write, throwing more emphasis on character development. If we believe in the characters, Grant asserts, that will enable us to overcome our disbelief of what is portrayed as happening in their lives.

The concerns expressed above are evident in Grant's fiction. His characters are clearly people about whom Grant himself cares. The protagonists of many of his novels are in some ways almost interchangeable. They tend to be younger adults, usually single women, with ambitious personal plans and a sense of independence. Frequently they are recently established in a business of their own, a bookstore, a toy shop, a librarian considering changing her job. The female protagonists usually have a male friend, although the romantic element is generally minimal. In fact, the male companions ultimately cannot help during the resolution of the main conflicts, and the protagonist is generally thrown back upon her own resources.

Grant's novels tend to follow a pattern of slow escalation. He builds mood not by introducing clanking chains, graphically depicted monsters, and the usual trappings of horror fiction, but in a far quieter and ultimately more effective fashion. With a series of small, mildly disturbing incidents, he disrupts the life of his characters enough that they begin to wonder what is going on in their world, or with his or her own mind, consequently unsettling the reader as well. Some of these devices are fairly traditional, some not, and they recur throughout his work: missing or mysteriously deceased animals, disturbing dreams, mysterious silent figures, unusual temperature extremes, disorientation, inexplicable phone calls, fumbled keys at doorlocks, or a persistent feeling of being observed. Frequently his characters begin to wonder if they are reacting to non-existent stimuli, that everything bizarre is occurring in their mind. Grant alludes to this theme in the introduction to *Shadows 5*: "The fascination, then, lies not in the insanity itself but in the possibility that the insanity can be so powerful as to create a new segment of reality—not just for the afflicted character, but for the others who inhabit that character's world as well." Presumably, since the reader will temporarily inhabit that world, our own view of reality can be affected as well.

Grant's first horror novel, *The Curse*, appeared in 1977, a not particularly successful book but one which foreshadowed much of the technique of developing suspense and mood that he refined in this later novels. A young couple moves into their new home in the suburbs and begins the process of blending into the neighborhood. Although ostensibly a normal community into which they are readily accepted, there are some slight peculiarities. Someone, for example, seems to be actively slaughtering all of the small animals in the area.

An odd phone call during a blizzard may or may not be a malfunction in the telephone lines. There are hints of an ancient Indian curse.

The protagonist is the young wife, whose desire to be accepted is at odds with her mild aversion toward some of her neighbors and her increasing uneasiness as the days pass. She discovers a mysterious marker in the woods, and is troubled by disturbing dreams. There is one quite effective scene where she becomes disoriented within her own home. Unfortunately, the plot does not develop well and the evocation of ancient Indian warriors in the final chapter doesn't work at all.

Happily, Grant put that novel behind him and produced six subsequent ones, each set in the town of Oxrun Station, a mythical community in Connecticut which may one day rival Arkham and Dunwich. Although not a series as such, characters from some of these books make cameo appearances in others, which provides a certain degree of continuity.

The first of these was *The Hour of the Oxrun Dead*, which opens with a scene that is typical of Grant's approach to grisly events. A policeman is lured to a remote site by a mysterious phone call, at which point he is murdered in a particularly brutal fashion. Our attention is directed to the bizarre nature of his death rather than the details of dismemberment, all of which happen offstage. Grant's aversion to the type of gory description that is found in the works of John Saul and Graham Masterton, for example, does not mean that vicious death is absent from his fiction.

A series of odd events begins to affect the life of the victim's widow, initially touching her life only marginally (defilement of religious institutions in the community) but gradually more intrusive. Her job at the local library enables her to detect a macabre pattern in the theft of books; she notices that several members of the community wear identical rings; she experiences a shared hallucination with a friend. Eventually she begins to fear incipient insanity as she begins to interpret events as a plot directed against her personally. Fortunately, her resolve is reinforced when a male companion reveals that some paranormal force is affecting his perception in an attempt to remove him from Oxrun Station. Although the secret Satanist society of the novel is fairly obvious, the inevitable final confrontation is uncertain enough to maintain the reader's attention.

The Sound of Midnight is equally low key, and is developed in quite similar fashion. A young boy drowns mysteriously shortly after visiting the toy shop owned by the protagonist. She is in fact the first to reach the body, drawn by his calls for help. She is not satisfied that the drowning was normal, for it happened in very shallow water and in a remarkably short period of time. The peculiarities are emphasized by a cryptic visit from the boy's aunt, who seems unnaturally interested in his last conversation, and by rumors of strange bonfires in the night.

The suspense intensifies as the protagonist encounters dead animals, uneasy dreams, and keys fumbled in the darkness. During a scavenger hunt, she and her male friend are assaulted by flaming arrows in a darkened field, all evidence of which has disappeared by the following morning. Slowly there emerges the profile of a shadowy struggle between two supernatural forces, linked somehow to an elaborate chess set, amongst which the protagonist must struggle for survival and understanding.

A conspiracy features prominently in the third Oxrun Station novel as well. *The Last Call of Mourning* wasn't even packaged as a conventional horror novel, even though it is considerably more suspenseful and frightening than the first two. The main character is a young woman intent upon establishing her independence by running a small business of her own. Almost immediately, there is a series of apparent accidents designed to frighten or kill her, or at least to discourage her from remaining in the community. She is residing with her family after an absence of several years, but the lapse of time has made them strange to her, a strangeness that she dismisses at first as only natural, but which becomes disconcertingly persistent as time goes on.

Eventually she learns that each of her relatives has spent a period of time at a nearby experimental medical clinic, run by the unpleasant Dr. Kraylin. Her aversion to this man is aggravated rather than diminished when he revives her father from an apparently fatal heart attack. Her only close friend is neutralized in the struggle when he is hospitalized following a near-fatal automobile accident, and she is left alone to face the increasing strangeness of her family. There is a particularly effective scene in which a dead, single-winged bird attacks her. Grant also indulges his fondness for the inconclusive ending, in which we are not quite certain if evil has in fact been vanquished, which provides a lingering sense of unease.

The Grave is an even better novel. Once again, a series of bizarre but apparently unrelated incidents works to unsettle the life of the protagonist, this time a man who makes a living by locating obscure items for people. He is mysteriously attacked by a bird, someone vandalizes his office, and there is a strange tension between his girl friend and her father, which seems to involve an elderly woman who lives with them but never appears in public. Grant also conjures up one of his most macabre incidents for this novel, an automobile accident which results in an extra human arm, unrelated to any of the victims. As usual, the gore is de-emphasized and offstage.

The characters are particularly well drawn, evidence of Grant's increasing skill as a writer. The succession of strange events includes enigmatic disappearances of elderly people on their birthdays and a

84

hidden graveyard. The reader is swept inexorably toward the final revelation of what is actually taking place, culminating in a bittersweet ending. Even when good triumphs over evil in a Grant story, the triumph is not necessarily a pleasant one.

The best of the Oxrun novels is *The Bloodwind*. A young woman who is engaged in trying to establish a new department at the local college is suspected of complicity in the puzzling vandalization of a colleague's automobile. This event is foreshadowed for the reader by a minor vandalization of her own car, an incident which becomes foreboding only in retrospect. In many ways, Grant's supernatural intrusions are at their lightest in this novel, which relies far more on the state of the protagonist's mind than on physical events in her environment. Perhaps for this very reason, it is extremely effective and frightening.

The Soft Whisper of the Dead is the sixth Oxrun novel, and it steps entirely out of character for the author. In addition to the historical setting (the Presidency of James Garfield), it features traditional vampires and all the trappings of the conventional vampire adventure, with its inherent melodrama. Although he thereby proved that he can write this type of novel, it is a fairly predictable and not very satisfying work when compared to his more subtle and effect style used elsewhere.

His longest work to date is *The Nestling*, which is slightly more conventional than the Oxrun novels, but which still remains the distinctive Grant touch for understatement. A remote town in the Southwest is the focus of increasing tension between Amerindians and European-descended settlers. The Indians are attempting to purchase the land they lost generations before by buying up farms, which causes tension among the steadily decreasing non-Indian population. A series of violent deaths and disappearances does nothing to reduce the tension.

Speculation about the identity of the killer ranges from a conspiracy to the incursion of a maddened bear, as victims—both human and animal—are dismembered and horribly mangled. Grant allows the reader to be aware that a gigantic supernatural flying creature is involved, somehow connected with Indian legendry, but we don't actually see the menace until the final chapters. The interpersonal conflicts are quite well done; in fact, there often seems to be more threat from the human characters than from the nightflying monster.

Grant also wrote four neo-gothic romances under the name "Deborah Lewis," all of which utilize supernatural devices, although in each case there is ultimately a rationalization. In *Voices Out of Time* he uses all of the conventional devices—the ruined castle, the curse of a long-dead sorceress, ghostly visitations and phantom assailants, seances and coldspots. The werewolf legend is invoked in *The Eve of the Hound*, set on a southern plantation. *The Wind at Winter's End* features druidic rites and *Kirkwood Fires* involves a voodoo cult seeking immortality through human sacrifice. Although there is no true supernatural element in any of these novels, they all make extensive use of the traditional horror devices that are otherwise largely absent from Grant's fiction.

Most of Grant's short horror fiction can be found in three collections. *Tales From the Nightside*, which has appeared in hardcover only, is the most extensive of these containing stories set in Oxrun Station, as well as those set in another of his recurring localities, Hawthorne Street, and others unrelated. There is some overlap between this and another collection, *A Glow of Candles and Other Stories*, which contains several of his better science fiction tales as well. *Nightmare Seasons* is a collection of four original novelettes, each set in Oxrun Station.

The effectiveness of a particular horror device is often quite subjective despite the skill of the author; a reader who is at ease with spiders might be more frightened by a story about disorientation, for example. Grant makes uses of a variety of different potential threats rather than relying upon variations of the same theme. In "If Damon Comes" a young boy returns from the dead in a strange perversion of love that is quite chilling, definitely a story whose impact lasts beyond its own length. "The Gentle Passing of a Hand" is similar in effect. In this case, a young boy learns what appears to be an innocuous magic trick, but it turns out to be a variation of the classic tale of paradoxical horror, "The Monkey's Paw" by W.W. Jacobs.

Frequently Grant's short fiction provides a single lasting image. There is a race of ancient beings living under a boulder in "From All the Fields of Hail and Fire," who kidnap children for nefarious purposes. Magic figures prominently again in "The Three of Tens," wherein an enchanted artifact thrown into a river gives unnatural life to something which should have remained inanimate. Children are the perpetrators rather than the victims in "When All the Children Call My Name" and "Come Dance With me on My Pony's Grave." In the former, a group of young children use the magical corner of their playground as a device whereby to wreak vengeance on a group of older boys. Our sympathies lie with the supernatural agency in the latter, as a young Vietnamese boy calls upon his father's sorcery to avenge the death of his pony.

One of Grant's best short stories, "Hear Me Now, Sweet Abbey Rose," has been collected only in *A Glow of Candles and Other Stories*. Perverted love figures in this story as well. An older man is fiercely protective of his daughters, particularly Abbey Rose. After a violent encounter with a group of drunken men, the family is attacked and Abbey Rose is killed. Grief at his loss turns to horror as he realizes that just as he was reluctant to relinquish her to a life of her own, now her ghost is unwilling to relinquish its emotional hold upon him.

The uncollected World Fantasy Award winning story, "Quietly Now," is another atypical story, featuring a traditional vampire, but with a unique twist.

Nightmare Seasons contains four previously unpublished stories, each set in Oxrun Station, at intervals of ten years. Their cumulative impact is quite effective. In the first, a young woman is plagued by the amorous attentions of a young man who can transform himself into a gigantic serpent. Another tale involves two beings who appear to be mother and daughter, but are actually a manifestation of supernatural force. A motorcycle gang composed of corrupted human beings causes a series of grotesque deaths in another story, one that is far more explicitly violent than is usual in Grant's work. The book closes with a more typical story, wherein a young woman's life is twisted by a bizarre cloaked figure that may or may not be a figment of her imagination.

Recent horror fiction is replete with blood and gore, and it is an obvious testimony to Grant's skill as a writer that he has been successful despite his comparatively understated and subtle rendering of horror themes. His reputation as one of the more literate writers in the genre can only improve as his body of published works grows.

BIBLIOGRAPHY

The Curse. Major Books, 1977.
The Hour of the Oxrun Dead. Doubleday, 1977.
Voices Out of Time (as by Deborah Lewis). Zebra Books, 1977.
The Eve of the Hound (as by Deborah Lewis). Zebra Books, 1977.
Kirkwood Fires (as by Deborah Lewis). Zebra Books, 1978.
The Sound of Midnight. Doubleday, 1978.
The Wind at Winter's End (as by Deborah Lewis). Zebra Books, 1979.
The Last Call of Mourning. Popular Library, 1979.
The Grave. Popular Library, 1981.
Tales from the Nightside. Arkham House, 1981.
A Glow of Candles and Other Stories. Berkley Books, 1981.
The Nestling. Pocket Books, 1982.
Nightmare Seasons. Doubleday, 1982.
The Soft Whisper of the Dead. Donald M. Grant, 1982.
The Dark Cry of the Moon. Donald M. Grant, 1985.

RAMSEY CAMPBELL: AN APPRECIATION
by T.E.D. Klein

> -That was the first time you were afraid of noth-
> ing—that day when you were catching butterflies—when
> you had reached the patch of sunlight. You were not
> afraid in the shadow, but you were afraid in the sun.
> -The sunlight was still, desolate, and arid. And you
> knew that something huge was just behind you. You
> ran. You fell and cut your knee. You got up and ran
> again, panting, your heart thumping, much too fright-
> ened to cry.
> -But when you got home you cried. You cried for a
> long time; and you never told anybody why.
>
> —Jean Rhys
> *After Leaving Mr. Mackenzie* (1930)

This is a story of how a young man crawled out from under
H.P. Lovecraft's shadow, saw the sun, and wrote *Demons by Daylight*...

Back in 1969, after Arkham House had exhausted its supply of
Lovecraft fiction and had run through three volumes of miscellaneous
"Lovecraftiana," it dipped still further into the barrel and came out
with *Tales of the Cthulhu Mythos*, a collection of pastiches in the
Lovecraft tradition.

Most of them were simply embarrassing; as Mike Heron might
have put it, they knew all the words and they sung all the notes, but
they never quite got the song. Yet I recall that even the Lovecraftiest
of the tales, those truest of the original models, were somehow unsatisfying; forcing my way through them, trying hard to become excited,
I realized that what I missed most was not the Lovecraft style (which,
let's face it, is eminently imitable; indeed, several of the writers had
mimicked it to perfection) but rather the man's *name*. The reason is
simple: I suspect that for many of his readers, Lovecraft's life has
become as fascinating as his tales; and, knowing as we do of the man's
eccentricity, the loneliness, the suffering, the beliefs he held so deeply,
that very name "Lovecraft" above a story seems to stamp the work with
a kind of sincerity, the sense of its being an artifact, that gives him
the advantage over all his disciples.   ·

What this means is that the best of the pastiches—i.e., the most faithful—were unaccountably the worst. One might almost conclude, in fact, that as a literary form, the pastiche is really a close cousin to the translation (if temporal rather than spatial) and that it is, therefore, in the words of the adage, like a woman; the more beautiful, the less faithful; the more faithful, the less beautiful.

It isn't so surprising as it might seem, then, that of all the *Tales of the Cthulhu Mythos*, the most effective were those that departed most radically from the original Canon. The best of the lot—and certainly the most haunting—was a short piece called "Cold Print." The title itself, in its very understatement, stood out in contrast to all the Dwellers in Darkness, the Shadows from the Steeple, and the Shamblers from the Stars that proliferated throughout the book; and the story stood out even more.

It began, it's true, with one of those portentous epigraphs from a Forbidden Work—in this case something called the *Revelations of Glaaki*, Volume 12 (certainly the most unsavory title since *De Vermis Mysteriis*)—and, in fact, the quotation itself was even more portentous than most, claiming as it did that "even the minions of Cthulhu dare not speak of Y'golonac"—rather an arrogant assertion for a relative newcomer to make, reminding one of those billboard ads that heralded the movie *Mighty Joe Young: "Mightier, More Terrifying Than King Kong!!!."*

Happily, though, this unholier-than-thou air was dispelled by the story's opening sentence, in which a young schoolmaster with the disreputable name of Sam Strutt "licked his fingers and wiped them on his handkerchief." The tale went on to include such untraditional elements as sexual frustration, loneliness, and outright horniness; pornography of the kind known euphemistically as "discipline"; hints of homosexuality and pedophilia; allusions to Burroughs, Robbe-Grillet, Hubert Selby, Jr., and B-movies ("The neon sign outside the window of his flat, a cliché but relentless as toothache...garishly defined against the night every five seconds..."); the commercialization of Christmas, and the despair that only a holiday can breed; throwaway images both comical and bleak ("Once he met the gaze of an old woman staring down at a point below her window which was perhaps the extent of her outside world. Momentarily chilled, he hurried on, pursued by a woman who, on the evidence within her pram, had given birth to a letter of newspapers..."); one reference to an obscure dabbler in the occult named Roland Franklyn; to say nothing of such un-Lovecraftian details as bus fumes, slush, snot, and dogshit; all capped by one of the most breathtakingly gruesome endings I have ever read.

Save for that memorable finale, and the fact that the story was miserably proofread, this was hardly the kind of thing one would expect to find in a volume of Lovecraftiana. It was much too good. It seemed a product of that lonely land somewhere between *New Grub*

Street and the "New Town" of *Jubb* (two of my favorite British novels); it was a tale Lovecraft might have written if he'd had the benefit
of an excellent editor, if he'd survived into the fifties—and if he'd
been far, far more honest about himself.

The tale's author, one J. Ramsey Campbell, was listed in the
back of the book. It was noted, with old maidish redundancy, that he
had "the same background as the popular Beatles—Liverpool, England,"
and that he had been born in 1946—a fact that must inevitably lead to
much consternation; it did, at least, in this writer, born but one year
later. One prefers one's heroes older.

The note went on to mention two books of Campbell's; one,
The Inhabitant of the Lake and Less Welcome Tenants, was, it declared, "published by Arkham House when he was but 18"—further
consternation and a gnashing of teeth!—and the other, *Demons by
Daylight*, was forthcoming.

There was obviously nothing else to do but send for that first
volume and wait for the second.

The former proved something of a let-down. Like Frank
Utpatel's rather cartoony cover and end-paper maps, the tales seemed
too eager to spell everything out. They told too much. So did the
introduction, in which the young author announced, with bold naivete,
his intention to create a new setting for the Cthulhu Mythos, the
Arkham area having been "saturated." (God knows he was right about
that!) He went on to describe each imaginary city in considerable
detail, as well as the "esoteric volume" from which he intended to
quote—thereby saving readers much work, but also much pleasure, a
mistake he was never to repeat. The effect was as if the bravado of
"Cold Print"'s epigraph had found its way into the text. That story had
been searingly honest about the secret urges of its protagonist; here,
unfortunately, the Campbell of an earlier day was proving all too can-
did about his own authorial ambitions.

Throughout the book one was conscious of a deliberate striving
after a Lovecraft *corpus*, a deliberate dropping of names, a deliberate
setting up of the horrors. Except for one understated little piece
called "The Will of Stanley Brooke," done largely in dialogue, the stories seemed filled with artifice; Campbell hadn't yet learned to cover
his tracks.

That it was an extraordinary work for an 18-year-old boy to
have produced was, of course, obvious in every line; but obviously,
too, this was the work of a writer still laboring in Lovecraft's shadow.

As I recall, probably the most interesting thing about the book
was the author's photo on the end-flap. Describing him as "one of the
youngest and most promising recruits to the domain of the
macabre"—as if the entire field were some colossal boys' club (and
perhaps it is) or the refuge of some crackpot pressure group (and perhaps it is)—the picture showed a gloomy-looking youth with plastic

glasses and short hair, very British public school-looking in a sweater, jacket and tie. His expression was both sullen and amused, with a slight touch of sneer, as if he'd really wanted to smile but was afraid it wouldn't do for a horror writer to look too jolly (a quite reasonable consideration). He looked like a boy who could be guilty of anything: the face of a mathematics prodigy, a child molester, or simply a repressed Catholic schoolboy gone wrong. It was obvious from his serene expression and level gaze that he had impure thoughts, and often. He looked, in a word, creepy. Which is to say, he was one of us.

In succeeding years other Arkham House editions were sent for, as finances and enthusiasms dictated. One by one the Derleth anthologies arrived, each with its spurious "unpublished Lovecraft" tale written by Derleth himself, testifying less to his modesty than to his marketing sense; and each time the first thing I looked for was the Campbell offering. He made, I believe, every volume.

They were a mixed bag. If no story ever excited me quite as much as "Cold Print," largely because of that one's unusually evocative atmosphere, they were nevertheless far superior to those tales in the *Inhabitant* volume. "The Church in High Street" was, to be sure, an example of Early Campbell, bearing that period's distinguishing feature, the over-explicit first-person narrator; it seemed, in fact, to belong more to *Inhabitant* than "The Will of Stanley Brooke," and no doubt preceded that tale. "The Stone on the Island" seemed heavy-handed too, but the story did offer pleasant hints of things to come: a protagonist desperately alone, his alienation seeming to distort the workaday world around him, rendering it surreal, dismal, absurd; the half-hearted passes at girls in the office; the office itself, convincingly dull, filled with obtuse people doing trivial things; and the conclusion, whose grisliness made up for whatever lapses the plot may have had.

"The Cellars," "Napier Court," "The Scar"—the tales grew better and better with each new volume, more subtle and more difficult. "Cold Print," I began to realize, had been a kind of Campbell primer, containing nearly all the elements that distinguished these later stories. The Early Campbell was gone, and so was the *corpus* he'd tried to create; at last we were witnessing the formation of a genuine body of work, unified not by mere intention but by vision.

That observation, of course, is one calculated to embarrass any writer, and to Campbell himself I apologize for it; it sounds entirely too grandiose, too pretentious. Yet a vision there was, a sustaining one; and with the publication of *Demons by Daylight* we saw that this vision of the universe—paranoiac, often confounding, always haunting, dreadful, unique—had been sustained throughout an entire book.

It was, to say the least, quite an event.

Judging from the several reviews I saw at the time, a lot was made of the book's cover by, we are told, "the eminent British artist and illustrator, Eddie Jones." It was, in fact, a very good one, and particularly appropriate: an attractive young girl, head up, hair frazzled and free, mouth agape, stands before us in a state of either awe, terror, or sexual excitation, wearing only a thin dress (through which, when you hold the book up to a strong light and squint ever so slightly, you can see her nipples) and a large ornamental cross—useless, we may be sure, against the insectoid demon skull that's superimposed over her.

The back cover too, is of interest: Campbell himself adorns it, looking very cocky and self-assured. In the earlier pose he had looked like a fan—the kind of photo one sees reproduced in the letter columns of monster magazines, complete with boasts about the subject's age; now, however, he looked more like a writer. Somewhere along the way between the two collections the "J." had been dropped from his name—shed, perhaps, like a caterpillar skin when he crawled out from beneath Lovecraft's shadow and took flight on his own—but the lack is more than made up for by a cascade of hair as long as the girl's on the front of the book. He has acquired, too, a new pair of glasses (still plastic, but better-looking), a black turtleneck sweater (the kind Colin Wilson wears in most of his pictures), and a wife—the former Jenny Chandler. (One might expect that after marriage his stories would have changed, his lonely heroes growing less haunted, less horny, to be ultimately replaced by cool, pipe-puffing Carnacki types...Happily, though, this does not seem to have occurred.) Campbell's sneer has grown; so, too, has his smile, though it's still knowing rather than welcoming. Standing with arms folded in the Liverpool Public Library (where he has worked), he holds—as if for display, or as a gratuitous plug—a book whose title is maddeningly hard to read; it seems to be *The House on the*—what? *Brink?* (+It is *The House on the Brink* a story for teenagers by John Gordon; -MA+) I can't help thinking this book, which I don't recognize, must be of vital importance—perhaps readers will enlighten me. (Still, I'm disappointed that it wasn't a copy of his imaginary Roland Franklyn's *We Pass From View.* This might have recalled the Brown University library's Lovecraft exhibit, arranged by Professor Barton Levi St. Armand, in which one of the airtight glass display cases contained, or so the card declared, "the legendary *Necronomicon*"—a fat, sinister-looking volume, unfortunately lying shut, the leather of the spine having long since rotted away.)

One of the first things that struck one about Campbell's stories in this new collection was that—following the trend of his earlier pieces—they are extremely difficult. In fact, let's not mince words: I found them hard as hell. More often than not I came to the end without realizing it, turning the page only to find myself faced with a new story, rather like those cartoons in which a man walking the plank strides several feet in the air before realizing he's gone past the end of the board. Frequently I had to retrace my steps, rereading the last few pages to see what I'd missed; on two occasions I remained still baffled, and my girlfriend had to explain the endings to me—demonstrating her own patience and, I suppose, the fact that I'm as obtuse as any of Campbell's Brichester revenue clerks.

Still, being "difficult" is not necessarily a fault; and for horror, in fact, it is almost always a great virtue. Several years ago, when I was teaching school, a fellow teacher was charged with being "too difficult" for the students; the material he presented was, it was argued, "over their heads." I recall his reply: "I think it's important to give them a little more than they can handle," he said. "I like to remain a little beyond them."

For an English instructor this may or may not be true; but for a horror writer, it should probably be the rule. Writing horror stories must be rather like playing the Pied Piper; if the tune one pipes is too fast or difficult or subtle, the reader grows bored and drops out of the dance. If, on the other hand, the tune is too plodding and predictable, the reaction is the same: boredom, loss of attention. The trick, apparently, is to dance just a little ahead of the reader, teasing him, leading him on.

The risk, of course, is considerable: if one balks at making the slightest concession to the reader, one may end up with a kind of "horror tale as minimal art," akin to the most progressive of progressive jazz or the most abstract of abstract painting. In that case, as Kirby McCauley has pointed out, one runs the risk of writing stories for oneself alone; even if other readers might have the means to decipher them, no one will care to try.

Yet the other extreme presents an even graver danger: write a tale too easy to grasp and you allow the reader to realize he is more intelligent than the writer—something that, inexplicably, a brilliant man like Derleth permitted in his own dismayingly predictable Lovecraft pastiches.

Campbell, fortunately, seems to have mastered that trick of dancing just beyond our reach. Most of his stories have a hazy, dreamlike quality in which events are comprehensible when taken by themselves as discreet units, but in which they are piled upon one another so frantically that one gets lost in the swirl. Take, for example, the mad rush of images that we find at the beginning of "The Lost":

> It was in Rudesheim that I had my first important insight into Bill's character. The previous night, outside Koblenz, we had caught a bus in an unsuccessful attempt to find the town centre and when our three marks fare ran out had been abandoned in the country, by a filling station railed off by leaping brilliant rain. I'd been sure there had been hefty figures following us

as we walked into the stinging darkness—but Bill had seen a bus heading back to our hotel; he hadn't wanted a fight. So we'd joined the rest of our coach party that morning. Chairlifts were strung down a hillside of vineyards to Rudesheim; I stood up until Bill protested, although I had already seen that there could be no danger at all unless you fell on one of the vinepoles. Our courier led us down into Rudesheim, through the contorted cobbled streets of aproned women selling souvenirs, between tables full of tankards and huge packed laughing Germans, and into an inn. Here Bill revealed himself.

Quite an opening paragraph—by no means Campbell's best writing, of course, but typical of the way he buffets the reader with a succession of unrelated images, so that one finds oneself growing winded, a little punchy—and at the same time more susceptible to Campbell's attack. Or (to mix metaphors) one cries, "Slow down!" but the tour has moved on, back to Rudesheim.

The fact that all these incidents are crowded into a single paragraph (the journalist in me would run them down the page) makes the writing seem even more compressed and difficult than it really is; often entire conversations receive the same treatment, with considerable atmospheric effect, if technically improper. Anyway, it all saves space and, one assumes, publishing costs. Furthermore this effect is compounded by the very size of the typeface used—abnormally tiny for an Arkham House edition. I suppose this minuscule type is as symbolic of this collection as Utpatel's thick heavily drawn lines were of the previous one.

Add to this the fact that, whether or not Campbell intended it, the tales are almost totally lacking in line breaks, and you have something very confusing indeed. One example from among dozens: in "At First Sight" we follow the heroine onto a bus: "As she passed the seat where she'd seemed to see the face she stretched out her hand and touched the leather. It was cold as the stones of a well." The new paragraph begins immediately: "A glass was held toward her, half-full of some dark liquid." Huh? Where, on the bus? Coca-Cola vendor, perhaps? But no: "Her eyes refused to look beyond the hand which held the glass. Then she saw that it was not a glass; it was a girl, struggling among her fingers, one bare arm thrust out beneath the thumb. Nor was it a hand that held her." And then a third paragraph: "Val sat up in bed." Etc. Somehow we've jumped from the bus-seat into a bed, after having plunged through a most confusing dream. My own belief is that Campbell made some allowance for a break after that first paragraph but that Arkham House ignored it; and it's probably significant that in the first issue of *Whispers* Stuart Schiff alluded to some "errors on the part of the printer" (perhaps he means the typeface) that marred production of this book. At any rate, this is one of the few times that sloppy printing has tended to accentuate the atmosphere of the stories.

The hand holding the glass that turns into a hand holding a girl ("Nor was it a hand that held her.") typifies another characteristic of Campbell's fiction: distorted images, seen always through the eyes of the protagonist, images that tend to shift and disappear as we try to understand them. "Their heads—no, they couldn't be heads," realizes one character. "On their shoulders were set huge paper masks like balloons, nodding horribly, their grinning mouths stretched wide as if bloated from within...Heads inflated by mud." That comes from a nightmare in "The Old Horns," but the images need not be confined to dreams. For example, in a city at night: "I saw a totem-pole striding toward me down a side-street. It was a child stacked on his father's shoulders." In "Concussion," a sentimental science fiction story reminiscent of Robert F. Young, based on a kind of nostalgia for the present, we find: "A colossal green leper stood on the horizon; the Liver Clock, flaking off each second from the future." Or, from a pub scene in "Made in Goatswood": "His face swam forward through the yellow light like a shark closing for the kill." And a few lines down: "Footsteps plodded up the stairs toward them. It was her father. Kim watched, unwillingly fascinated. The father took shape from the shadows, looming above them. The footsteps continued." It is as if we've been forced to look at the world through a fish-eye lens, or the spectacles of some astigmatic stranger. People dream, even in daylight; they are prone to visions any place they go—city streets, even—and thus any place can be frightening. It's a world in which a totem-pole can come striding down the sidewalk toward you, and even after it's been "explained away" the surreal quality lingers. In short, it's a world in which anything can happen. Expect anything. Expect the worst.

What this leads to is a kind of dream-like paranoia that affects his characters' perceptions—not a new thing for horror stories, it's true, except that Campbell does it so much better, and he does it in crowds more often than not. In the paragraph I quoted from "The Lost," one of the first things the narrator mentions is the "hefty figures following us as we walked into the stinging darkness;" and later in that same tale, the narrator finds himself in a German tavern, staring at a girl at the bar: "I was fascinated," he reports. "She seemed to be with three overflowing men. She must have known when eyes were watching her wherever they were, just as I do, for she turned and stared at me...She said something to the man on her right, and he swung round trailing smoke, his cigar like a blackened gun-barrel, to train his gaze on me. I knew he was hostile; I always do."

Admittedly the tale presents us with a patently insane narrator whose vision of the universe is deliberately distorted; but such distortion is the norm throughout this book. (And for all the narrator's paranoic delusions, events bear out his philosophy: a mere flood of German curses provokes the longed-for murder of his companion.)

One effect of this distorted vision is that the reader becomes even more paranoiac than the protagonist: after reading several Campbell stories, one's ear grows extraordinarily sensitive to conversations overheard at the next table (something about that girl they found dead in the park...), and one learns to pay scrupulous attention to stray scraps of wind-tossed newspaper bearing ominous references to "mutilations" and "police baffled...". The ladies on the bus, one seat behind us, are talking about a series of murders, and we find ourselves nodding cynically—"Uh-huh, somebody's going to *get* it!"—aware as we are that Campbell is above all an economical writer, and that half-heard conversations and muttered warnings are seldom inserted simply as window dressing; they are *clues* and, like as not, the protagonist—who ignores them—is going to wind up just as mutilated as the corpse the news vendor hinted of...

But stray snatches of bar-room conversation are by no means required to raise the hackles of a veteran Campbell reader; simple code words are often enough. Shadows, gloom, an alley, a deserted park on an evening in February, a row of abandoned warehouses—we don't ask for much. A cave, perhaps, as in the brilliant "End of a Summer's Day," but that's hardly necessary—a mere hint of underground passages, a dark doorway that might perhaps lead to catacombs, a trap-door in the floor of a basement...No need for elaboration, no need for mapping out the subterranean network of tunnels (a Campbell staple). Just give us the doorway or the trap-door, and we'll fill in the rest. After all, we've been here before.

Such is the cumulative power of the best horror fiction—Lovecraft's, Machen's, and certainly Campbell's. Each new tale gains drama and atmosphere from those that have gone before—which, of course, gives writers such as Campbell an immediate edge over newcomers to the field. Take a story by an unknown writer and, if it opens with a picnic on the beach, we'll be yawning by page two. After all, an ordinary summer's outing...what's scary about that? Who cares if the title is "The Slime Monster" or something equally lurid? Yet Campbell can rivet our attention with just such a scene, and we'll react with a shudder to every mention of dunes and mud-puddles—despite a title as innocuous as "The Old Horns."

That may be one reason why the genre tends to spawn such apparent "addicts"—and conversely why the uninitiated reader who comes upon some classic horror tale for the first time may well react with little more than boredom: up to a certain point (after which, we may suppose, the returns begin to diminish), the effect of horror is cumulative. Which isn't to say that one should read through *Demons by Daylight* at one sitting—that would be an unfortunate mistake, akin to gorging oneself on a pound of 'macadamia nuts. The individual stories are too rich, and need a day or two for the psyche to digest.

Campbell's readers, then, become acutely sensitive to phrases that evoke atmosphere, as well as to carefully placed hints of imminent doom. As with most horror stories, the reader is customarily one step ahead of the protagonist, leading to a kind of reluctant fascination, the old "Don't-go-in-there-you-fool" syndrome—for, of course, the hero does go in there, and ultimately pays for it.

The fact that so many Campbell heroes end up dead suggests that Campbell's universe is not a particularly moral one; innocent people are just as prone to die as the guilty, and that Campbell primer, "Cold Print," ends on just such a note: "Strutt's last thought was an unbelieving conviction that this was happening because he had read the *Revelations*; somewhere, someone had *wanted* this to happen to him. It wasn't playing fair, he hadn't done anything to deserve this—but before he could scream out his protest his breath was cut off..."

No, it isn't particularly fair; Campbell's obsessive young men and neurotically passive young women don't deserve to die. And yet, in a sense, all of them are guilty of *something*—an overweening curiosity, perhaps, or, as in Strutt's case, simply "evil thoughts." I can't help but wonder (as one is supposed to wonder in essays like this) if such retribution isn't some sort of holdover from Campbell's Catholic upbringing; Catholicism is, after all, a religion that punishes one for sinful thoughts as well as sinful actions. We are, in that case, all of us guilty.

Not that the Church represents any "Force of Goodness" in these stories. It seems, in fact, rather impotent, indeed quite fatuous: a collection of lithograph Jesuses and a herd of sheep trotting into a cathedral. (This image, from Bunuel's *The Exterminating Angel*, represents one of Campbell's many film references; for that matter his very narrative makes frequent use of cinematic devices: a hideous face at the window, out of focus, is revealed as a friend; flash cuts to the details of a city street yield a kind of cinematic fragmentation, etc. Campbell has, in fact, written film criticism for the BBC.)

When it comes to Catholicism I'm out of my depth, so I'd prefer to leave heavy analyses of "Good vs. Evil in the Campbell Oeuvre" to future generations of grad students; but it is worth pointing out that such a conflict doesn't even exist in these tales. There *is* no force of goodness to pit against evil; we are given no heroic Dr. Armitages or Professor Rices to battle against Campbell's Yog-Sothoths. In fact, Campbell eschews heroes of any kind; many of his creations are criminal, and the rest enjoy a stature no better than our own: they are weak, timid, and—if in love—selfishly so. Were they suddenly to receive "magical powers," they'd certainly abuse them. They are, in short, refreshingly easy to identify with, after years of cool-eyed psychic investigators and aristocratic aesthetes.

Ironically, the only force arrayed against the sundry evils of the universe is the force of human stupidity. By that I mean the very blindness, insensitivity, slavishness to habit and dogma, that keeps Campbell's minor characters busy with their daily rounds in the office while the protagonist is going quietly mad from fear. The effect is, once again, very dreamlike, for if the reader customarily knows more than the main character, *he* in turn knows a great deal more than the minor ones, and therefore finds himself in that horrifyingly familiar world in which no one but himself quite understands what's going on. Such paranoia reaches its height in "The End of a Summer's Day," one of those perfect stories that, like Lovecraft's "Hypnos" and "Polaris," allows for two satisfactory sets of explanations: one quite natural, one less so. On the one hand it's the apotheosis of that infantile nightmare, "I'm screaming and no one's listening," and in fact it appears in the section Campbell labels "Nightmares" (perhaps we should take him at his word). On the other hand, one can't help theorizing the existence of strange subterranean cults who, for reasons of their own, inhabit certain English caves where, every ten years or so, they trap a luckless tourist, substituting for him their previous captive—who, by this time, is as blind as a mole.

Exasperating as they are, these herds of common humanity with their heads stuck in their newspapers—muttering about "all this godlessness going round" and "Don't get involved" and other banalities—do constitute a kind of strength, running their sane little world in the midst of a mad universe. "What do you believe in?" asks a Campbell hero, and his girlfriend's father answers, quite seriously, "What's around me. Not politics disguised as panaceas, not poets trying to be philosophers. This house. My job. Reality." One senses a kind of wisdom here, in this middle-class sage; it's obvious that he speaks from long experience. Believe deeply enough in your slogans, and nothing can harm you...(One senses too, Campbell's ambiguity toward the character; he's given him some good lines.) At any rate, it isn't the people like him who get hurt: it's the meddlesome few who learn, as in Lovecraft, More Than Mortals Were Meant to Know. They pay for it, these characters, in suffering and death; and those who aren't killed find their perceptions of the world forever altered.

If darkness is to be defeated, then, it won't be by any mystical Powers or Catholic saints; it will be by unimaginative men keeping their minds on their work. Thus the slogan might run, "In Banality There Is Strength"—but that doesn't really offer much protection. The title, *Demons by Daylight*, notwithstanding, there isn't any light in Campbell's world to hold back the darkness; and this does tend to make the tales inexorably grim and pessimistic. Lovecraft, at least, offered a wide variety of panaceas: Science, The Great Race, Childhood, Dreams, the very concept that "It's All in Your Mind" (a la *Kadath*) and hence not to be feared. In the world of M.R. James there's a kind of Victorian social stability to rescue us from ancestral ghosts; one flees the cemetery or the swamp and returns to a comfortable seat by the fire. And Arthur Machen balances his pagan atrocities with hymns to pagan joy; to use Walter Van Tilburg Clark's phrase, Machen gives us both "the ecstasy and the dread." But in Ramsey Campbell's world, there is only the dread.

It's absurd, of course, to take a horror writer to task for writing horror, especially when he does it with such originality and grace; indeed, I think Campbell reigns supreme in the field today. Yet horror *per se* can be, in the end, somewhat limiting; and now that he has mastered it, one might hope for an occasional ray of light to alleviate the gloom. Black magic, by its existence, implies white magic; and while I'm not looking for a collection of fairy tales, it strikes me that an occasional vision of something beyond a glass of stout and a secretary's knickers might add a needed dimension to the world Campbell has created.

Parenthetically, though Campbell's world is far removed from that of M.R. James, he does seem to embody one of that scholar's most memorable virtues: he can create a monster in a single felicitous phrase. We've all read the famous "face of crumpled linen," but James has come up with other descriptions just as clever, such as this passage from "The Treasure of Abbot Thomas":

> Well, I felt to the right, and my fingers touched something curved that felt—yes—more or less like leather: dampish it was, and evidently part of a heavy, full thing...[He is attempting to pull a bag of gold from a hold in the side of a pit.TK] I pulled it to me, and it came. It was heavy, but moved more easily than I had expected...My left elbow knocked over and extinguished the candle. I got the thing fairly in front of the mouth and began drawing it out...I...went on pulling out the great bag, in complete darkness. It hung for an instant on the edge of the hole, then slipped forward on to my chest, and *put its arms round my neck.*

In "Napier Court" Campbell paints a similar image:

> Resting against the beacon was a white bag, half as high as Alma. She'd seen such bags before, full of laundry. Yet she could not force herself to pull back the gates and pass...the shapeless mass, for deep within herself

she suppressed a horror that the bag might move toward her, flapping.

"Flapping"—a perfect word, reminding one of the "horrible hopping creature in white" from James's "Casting the Runes," a creature "which you saw first dodging about among the trees, and gradually it appeared more and more plainly."
Words ending in "-ing" are clearly an effect device; "The Old Horns" offers "a prancing figure," and in "The Sentinels" Campbell uses one such word to bring the tale to a climax:

> "The face," Maureen sobbed, clutching Douglas...
> "Oh, God," Douglas shouted, "Barbara!"
> The car whipped about...and skidded into the road.
> A tunnel of trees sprang forth, into which it plunged. The figure ran alongside, skipping high.

As if this weren't enough, we get one more brilliant phrase—constituting our final sight of the thing:

> Ahead the tunnel of light dwindled: Barbara was gone.
> Only the last light of the car and, as it turned the corner, the shape which leapt easily onto the roof.

Hopping, skipping, prancing...All are deliberately innocuous words; so is "the shape which leapt easily onto the roof" (note the adverb), and the crack in the ceiling which "suddenly, with a horrid lethargy, detached itself from the plaster and fell on Peter's upturned face." The last is ostensibly an excerpt, the only one Campbell provides, from an apocryphal story by his creation, Errol Undercliffe. My only question is why, of all the possible lines to attribute to Undercliffe, he attributes one so characteristic of his own work ("with a horrid lethargy"—how perfect), and why, of all the stories in the book to bear Undercliffe's name, he has chosen "The Interloper"—a terrifying piece that, from catacombs to classrooms, bears the Campbell stamp in every line. It even reintroduces us to poor Sam Strutt.
Whatever Campbell's reasons for adopting this alter ego (it obviously isn't to write a kind of work alien to his own), both the story and the line are magnificent creations. I find the latter particularly memorable because it's precisely the sort of image that would "make" many a successful horror story—sometimes a good line is all that's really needed—and yet Campbell seems able to toss off such lines without half trying. (See, too, the marvelous twist in "The Second Staircase" as to the protagonist's sex, and how casually Campbell brings it off.) This easy facility, this feeling of "talent to spare," reminds me of the baseball star Stan Musial who, when asked what he would do if

he suddenly found himself in a batting slump, replied (after a long pause and much head-scratching), "Well, I can always hit to third." He meant that, even on the worst of days, he could always get on base. For any player of even normal ability, that would have been an impossible boast; for Musial it was a simple statement of fact. Campbell's ability seems just as extraordinary; judging from his recent work, "he can always write scary." How many other young writers can say the same?

However, if we're going to honor Campbell—and that's what this essay is all about—it should be not so much for his style as his content. As his own short career demonstrates, he has changed the shape of the modern horror story; he has done for our own field what other young British writers are doing for science fiction. And for a one-time Lovecraft disciple to have done so is all the more impressive; it's as if E.E. Smith had suddenly begun producing self-referential literary experiments in the style of J.G. Ballard.

Best of all, he has made the horror story relevant (a word that, quite rightly, makes everyone wince). At last, in *Demons by Daylight*, we have a volume in which the hero is convincingly human, not a neurasthenic antiquarian or a gentleman of leisure or a mad scientist or an eccentric sculptor. We have, instead, a fellow who works in a boring office or library and who wishes he had time to read *The Golden Bough* but hasn't gotten around to it yet. He wishes, too, that he were more clever, so that he could impress the girls at the office; he'd willingly (and on occasion, literally) stab his best friend in the back for a chance to snake his girlfriend. He desperately needs women, and longs for them; he also loathes, fears, and despises them. ("Women—he hated them, their soft helpless bodies, passively resisting, unattainable."—"The Second Staircase.") Like her male counterpart, the Campbell heroine spends a great deal of her time feeling lonely, wishing she looked as sexy as her flatmate, wondering how far she should let that new boy go with her, wondering if that fellow she met in the pub will call her like he said...

If such characters seem real and ordinary and (at times) embarrassingly easy to identify with, it's because in every story Campbell appears to have risen to a challenge; he's taken a dare, broken a rule, violated a taboo. In regard to characters, this challenge may be unstated, but implicit in the long horror tradition: that one's protagonists must be exotic creatures without genitals or neuroses. In regard to setting atmosphere, the challenge may be spelled out:

> No author...can conceive of the difficulty of writing a romance about a country where there is no shadow, no antiquity, no mystery, no picturesque and gloomy wrong, nor anything but a commonplace prosperity, in

broad and simple daylight...Romance and poetry, ivy, lichens, and wallflowers need ruin to make them grow.

So declares Hawthorne in *The Marble Faun*, and so declares Isaac Bashevis Singer in our own day:

> Even if demons do exist, they are not in New York. What would a demon do in New York? He could get run over by a car or tangle himself in a subway and never find his way out.
> —"Lost," *The New Yorker*, 23 June 1973

One might almost suspect Campbell had read such assertions—No daylight! No demons in the city!—and had dedicated his career to disproving them. *Demons by Daylight* was the result, and a success.

JAMES HERBERT: NOTES TOWARD
A REAPPRAISAL
by Ramsey Campbell

"James Herbert," Stephen King writes in *Danse Macabre*, "is held in remarkably low esteem by writers in the genre of both sides of the Atlantic." I was one of the writers he had in mind. A thorough reading of Herbert's work has convinced me I was wrong, and I've begun to wonder if Herbert is disliked by some writers because he challenges the class bias of English horror fiction.

English horror fiction is almost entirely middle-class, either in its overt attitudes or its assumptions. As the world outside this perimeter becomes increasingly difficult to ignore, writers react in various ways: Dennis Wheatley blamed everything that threatened his way of life on Satan; Basil Cooper retreats consciously to the Victorian era and writes, as one reviewer aptly put it, "as if he lived in a timeless void of writing." Compared with the American tradition, English horror fiction is singularly lacking in working-class characters, and too many of those it presents are caricatures: for example, Brian Lumley's criminals (one of whom manages to call a character both "guv" and "recluse") ring as false as Russell Wakefield's. All too often the working class in English genre fiction seem based on versions of the working class received from English genre fiction. Not so with James Herbert, whose first novel *The Rats* (1974) is based solidly in the real world.

In this novel a mutant strain of rats bred in the East End of London emerges from a derelict house to hunt human beings. The threat is eventually contained by government intervention, though not, as the sequel *Lair* makes clear, for very long. Herbert himself was born and bred in the East End, in a street which had been left half derelict by bombing, and which was overrun by rats. The protagonist of the novel, a teacher called Harris, has a background that resembles Herbert's. "How colourful," an art student remarks about Harris's East End background; perhaps it was this kind of comment that encouraged Herbert to show the area as it really was.

The Rats announces at once that he won't be confined by the conventions of English macabre fiction. The first chapter is a sympathetic portrait of an alcoholic who has become outcast because of his homosexuality, while the fifth portrays one of several derelicts who

103

meet on a bomb site. This latter chapter has a savage power that recalls *Last Exit to Brooklyn*, and as in Selby's novel, aesthetic objections to the savagery are beside the point: it would be dishonest of both writers to try to soften their material so as to spare the reader. In Herbert's case, given that he was working in the mid-seventies in a genre often dictated to by the audience's expectations, his refusal to mince the squalor is all the more admirable.

The rats "were the system," Herbert said in an interview for *Fangoria* magazine. "That's why it was open ended, the system still goes on." They clearly also represent neglect personified. "What disgusted him more?" Harris the teacher reflects. "The vermin themselves—or the fact that it could only happen in East London?" But Harris continues "It was no good becoming over-wrought with authority, for he knew too well that apathy existed on all levels...Wasn't that what Original Sin was supposed to be about? We're all to blame..." That the book can discuss its underlying themes so directly without becoming pretentious—a trap into which several contemporary American writers in the field have fallen—is one of Herbert's strengths. The hint of Catholicism is developed in later books, while the flaws of "the system" are explored in more detail in his next book, *The Fog* (1975).

The fog is a bacteriological weapon, stored underground when its development was discontinued, released by the army's testing explosives. Herbert uses the situation of a potentially nationwide disaster for two purposes: to show its effect on ordinary people and how they respond (as in the science fiction novels of H.G. Wells and, later, John Wyndham) and to illuminate flaws in the Establishment, particularly in terms of the way they deal with the crisis (a tendency in Herbert's writing which recalls the Quatermass stories of Nigel Kneale). In Herbert's work, however, the "ordinary" person is generally lonely and often deeply flawed. Portraits of loneliness are central to almost all his novels (some of the most extreme appearing in the early chapters of *The Rats*), and the typical Herbert hero is an outsider who develops a strong, usually sexual, relationship in the course of the novel.

Where *The Rats* had its characters doing their best to cope with a crisis, *The Fog* shows its characters invaded by the threat, a "fog" or gas which causes insanity. (In this it resembles Charles Platt's' pornographic novel *The Gas*, but Herbert's novel is altogether more controlled.) The book has been criticized for the consequent scenes of violence, and Stephen King quotes Herbert as saying that his approach to writing it was "I'm going to try to go over the top, to see how much I can get away with" (a comment reminiscent of Straub's statement that he meant *Ghost Story* to "take the classic elements of the horror novel as far as they could go"). But *The Fog* contains remarkably few graphic acts of violence, though two (in a gymnasium and in the bedroom of a Chief Superintendent of police) are so horrible and painful,

at least for this reader, that they pervade the book. Herbert concen-
trates rather on painting a landscape of (occasionally comic) nightmare,
and most of the human episodes are of terror rather than of explicit
violence: the pilot of a 747 goes mad at the controls, and in the most
disturbingly ironic scene, a would-be suicide who has thought better
of making away with herself is caught up in a lemming-like exodus
from the seaside town of Bournemouth. Herbert triumphantly reverses
the usual method of building terror in a novel: where traditionally this
is achieved by a gradual accumulation of events, *The Fog* is all the
more nightmarish for its breathless pace. Its final image (prefiguring
that of the film *Alien*) is, appropriately, of restful sleep.

The Fog was a best-seller, but Herbert's next two books show
that he won't play safe. *The Survivor* (1976)—later filmed, insipidly
and obscurely, by David Hemmings—is the pilot of a 747, the only
person to survive its crash, who proves to have been sent on a mission
by the spirits of its victims. Though the book rises to heights both of
horror (an infernal scene in a college chapel) and ecstasy, it's weighed
down by too much spiritualistic discussion, as hindering to Herbert as
it was to Algernon Blackwood. Perhaps at the time Herbert's preoccupation with the afterlife, or his doubts about life after death, was so
great that the theme got the better of him. For most of its length *The
Survivor* (an ironic title) is among his bleakest books, not least because
the pilot's lover has been killed in the crash.

Fluke (1977) returns to the subject of the afterlife, but with
greater stylistic and narrative confidence. Of all his books, this
divides his admirers most sharply; none of his books conforms less to
the expectations of his fans. Fluke is a man reincarnated as a dog,
much to the dismay of Herbert's British publishers, who would have
preferred the dog at least to be rabid. It is Herbert's only first-person
narrative so far, and it may be this unaccustomed voice that reveals
new qualities—a greater generosity toward his characters, an unexpected lyricism. Significantly, it's his favourite among his novels. Not
that the book is inconsistent with his other work: again the protagonist
(in many ways the typical Herbert hero) is sent on a quest whose outcome proves to be ironic. A greater belated irony may be that the
entire book-length monologue goes unheard by its chosen audience, a
dying tramp. However, the image of extreme loneliness gives way to a
finely suggestive last line.

If his next book, *The Spear* (1978)—an action thriller about
neo-Nazism and the resurrection of Himmler—is more immediately
commercial, nevertheless it's courageous of Herbert to address the
theme of British fascism through a genre which, like sword and sorcery, attracts fascist mentalities. (One of the most blatant statements
of this appears at the end of Dennis Wheatley's non-fiction coffee-
table book *The Devil and All His Works*, where Wheatley declares that
anti-apartheid demonstrations are the devil's work and that it is the

job of governments to govern.) *The Spear* scores as a thriller, especially in its set-pieces (a Herbert specialty, perhaps most skillfully and expressively employed in *The Fog*), but its anti-fascist message was clear enough to earn Herbert the hatred of the National Front, the British fascist party. Because the supernatural is only hinted at in the course of the novel, the climactic manifestation is the more disturbing.

Herbert sees *Lair* (1979), the sequel to *The Rats*, as a relaxation after *The Spear*. It attacks the apathy of officialdom with renewed vigour, and contains one of the most terrible death scenes in all his work, the death of a priest who is losing his faith. This points forward to the more explicit horrors of *The Dark*.

The Dark (1980) is necessarily his most violent novel. Whereas the possessing force in *The Fog* was unmotivated, the dark is evil embodied and deliberately invoked. The book is about the rejection of God, whatever God may be. Proving the non-existence of God is seen as the ultimate insanity; rejection of faith leads straight to breakdown and the asylum. *The Dark* conveys a greater sense of helplessness than Herbert's earlier work; the little-organized response to the threat is largely ineffectual. It's to his credit that he doesn't use the theme of possession as an alibi for his characters (which is to say, to allow the reader to feel that evil has nothing to do with us). The novel's most terrifying scene, an outbreak of football hooliganism, is shown hardly to need possession to cause it at all.

The Jonah (1981) restates this theme in passing: a character dismisses the supernatural as "something people have invented to suit their own tiny minds, something that helps them put troubles and misfortunes into tiny little boxes." As in *The Spear*, the supernatural is kept largely offstage until the final chapters. The "jonah" is a policeman haunted by something that brings disaster to those involved with him and which he finally confronts while investigating drug smuggling. It's an oddly contradictory book: one character gives a speech against drug abuse so impassioned that it's reasonable to conclude (particularly since her partner in argument hardly gets a word in) that Herbert endorses her feelings, yet a later description of an LSD trip is as lyrical as it is terrifying. Presumably Herbert's imagination is stronger than his doubts. Still, *The Jonah* is his most lightweight book.

Shrine (1983) is an overtly Catholic novel, about a child who claims to have had a vision of the Virgin Mary but who is in fact inspired by the devil. The first half of *Shrine* is as compelling as any of his novels, and leads to a stunning set-piece that is rounded off by a breathtaking supernatural image. Untypically, the second half slows down enough to let the reader spot inconsistencies: symptoms of possession which the reader can't help but recognize seem to trouble the religious characters far less than they should (though this might be one of Herbert's objections to the way the Catholic church responds to the child's visions). Once again he uses the conventions of the genre more responsibly than many of his peers: there is no suggestion that the child herself is evil. Despite its flaws, *Shrine* is deeply felt and clearly was a book Herbert had to write, and some of its effects show a new deftness and subtlety. Some readers have found the final apparition ambiguous, but presumably Herbert is being true to his own doubts.

Domain (1984) is one of his most vividly imagined novels. It pits man against mutant rat in a London devastated by nuclear bombing. As in several of his novels, there are vignettes of character at the moment of disaster; those in *Domain*, and the insights they convey, are especially bleak. A scene in which characters try to clear an escalator piled with corpses has a nightmare absurdity, while the novel's sense of suffering is appropriately more intense than that of any of its predecessors. One chapter in which an injured man is dragged back from drowning is as disquieting as anything Herbert has yet given us. *Domain* is really only nominally a novel about the rats; it's a clear-eyed view of a future that may be uncomfortably close, and a praiseworthy attempt to give readers what they may not think they want.

Herbert writes best-sellers, but he doesn't manufacture them. Rather than compete with his imitators in terms of escalating violence (a trap into which such as John Carpenter and the EC comics of the fifties have fallen) he has opted for restraint. His sex scenes are sometimes prolonged, but they range from the tender to (particularly in *Shrine*) the grotesquely comic to an accumulation of awkward detail which is the opposite of pornographic. Some of his novels contain no sex at all. It may be his Catholicism, or the puritanism that seems to underlie *The Jonah*, which leads him to suggest that any kind of sexual deviation is bound for grief, but in other ways his work is less reactionary than much of the genre. While sometimes he stumbles stylistically, there's a developing sense of language in his effects. In *Danse Macabre*, in the course of an appreciation of Herbert, King describes him as coming at the reader "with both hands, not willing to simply engage our attention; he seizes us by the lapels and begins to scream in our faces. It is not a tremendously artistic method of attack, and no one is ever going to compare him to Doris Lessing or V.S. Naipaul...but it works...He is what he is and that's all that he is, as Popeye would say." To be fair, King has more to say for him than that, yet I wonder if some of King's readers may have gained the impression that Herbert's work is cruder than in fact it is. Herbert is an unmistakably English, and unmistakably contemporary, writer who refuses to conform to what's expected of him or to stop questioning what he sees and feels. I take his best books so far to be *The Fog*, *Fluke* and *Domain*, and I look forward to more surprises from him.

AMERICAN GOTHIC:
JOSEPH PAYNE BRENNAN
by Alan Warren

Joseph Payne Brennan is a poet, short story writer, novelist and editor whose macabre short fiction has generated acclaim from a small circle of aficionados for more than thirty years. Almost single-handedly, he continued the *Weird Tales* tradition of well-wrought and atmospheric Gothic horror that seemed moribund for many years until Stephen King, and others employing many of the same methods, arrived on the scene, at which point the pendulum began swinging back in the other direction. This has not affected Brennan, who continues to turn out short fiction at the same leisurely rate as always: he remains unknown to the general public but highly regarded by many of his better-known peers.

Brennan was born December 20, 1918, in Bridgeport, Connecticut. Shortly afterward his family moved back to New Haven, where he has lived ever since. He was forced to drop out of college in his sophomore year owing to an illness in the family; thus, he is largely self-educated. He began working at the Yale University Library in 1941; this was interrupted by military duty in the U.S. Army, where he earned five battle stars. He resumed work as acquisitions assistant at Yale in 1946, and published his first book, *Heart of Earth*, a poetry collection, in 1950. Arkham House brought out two collections of his short stories: *Nine Horrors and a Dream* in 1958, and *Stories of Darkness and Dread* in 1973. Macabre House also issued two collections: *The Dark Returners* (1959) and *Scream at Midnight* (1963). Berkley issued another, so far his only mass-market paperback, *The Shapes of Midnight* (1980). His stories about Lucius Leffing, psychic investigator and private detective somewhat in the tradition of William Hope Hodgson's Carnacki, have been collected in two volumes, *The Casebook of Lucius Leffing* (1973) and *The Chronicles of Lucius Leffing* (1977). He published two "little" magazines himself: *Essence* (1950-1977) and *Macabre* (1957-1976). His poetry, articles and short stories have appeared in numerous publications including *Weird Tales, Esquire, Alfred Hitchcock's Mystery Magazine, Southern Poetry Review, Mike Shayne Mystery Magazine, Western Short Stories, Commonweal* and *Reader's Digest*.

This multiplicity of literary roles does not seem unusual to Brennan. As he told *Contemporary Authors*: "After you've published for some time, readers and editors seem to demand that you fall into a definite—and largely inflexible—mold. You are a mainstream poet, or a horror-story writer, or a detective-story writer, or perhaps a so-called 'sword-and-sorcery' writer. I've always chafed under this categorizing. Why object if a poet writes short stories, or if a selling story writer decided to spend a year writing poetry?"

Brennan's earliest horror fiction was published in *Weird Tales* during its declining years, and most of his horror fiction, heavily influenced by Lovecraft, is in the tradition of that magazine. At that time, in the mid-1950s, the classical horror story was thought to be on its way out, forced to make room for science fiction and modern, "quiet" psychological horror fiction. Brennan persevered, and in a sense time has proved him right: Stephen King, for one, admits that Brennan is one of the writers he patterned his own career after. Brennan shares with King the ability to, as Peter Straub puts it, "describe the horror and put it right in front of your face," without its being laughably inadequate or overdone. Part of this is due to Brennan's simple style: his horrors are vivid because they stand out in sharp relief against his homespun, small-town scenes. As King notes, "you will find nothing flashy in his work...Brennan writes in what E.L. White called 'the plain style,' a style which is as modest and as self-effacing as Joe Brennan is himself...but for all of that, it is a sturdy style, capable of wielding enormous power when it is used well." To consider some typical stories (*Shapes of Midnight*, introduction, xii):

"Slime" is probably Brennan's best-known and most frequently anthologized story. It is the lead story in his collection *Nine Horrors and a Dream* (dedicated, appropriately enough, "To the memory of *Weird Tales*, 1923-1954"), and from its first sentences holds the reader in its strange power:

> It was a great gray-black hood of horror moving over the floor of the sea. It slid through the soft ooze like a monstrous mantle of slime obscenely animated with questing life. It was by turns viscid and fluid. At times it flattened out and flowed through the carpet of mud like an inky pool; occasionally it paused, seeming to shrink in upon itself...
>
> It was animated by a single, unceasing, never-satisfied drive: a voracious, insatiable hunger. It could survive for months without food, but minutes after

eating it was as ravenous as ever. Its appetite was appalling and incalculable." (*Nine Horrors*, pp. 3-4)

This *thing*, of course, goes on to devour many of the good citizens of Clinton Center after crawling out of Wharton's Swamp. The atmosphere conjured up by this community is decidedly cozy and small-town, almost Bradburyish. The plot is hardly remarkable, no more so than that of F. Marion Crawford's "The Upper Berth," which is often considered the most frightening ghost story in the English language. But both stories are undeniably effective.

"Levitation," though less horrific, is an ingenious little anecdote about a hypnotist performing his stage show at Morgan's Wonder Carnival in one of Brennan's typical small towns. The hypnotist, heckled by a young man in the crowd, invites him up on stage and puts him under a deep trance, then commands him to rise from the platform, unassisted by wires. Just as the young man begins to ascend horizontally, the hypnotist suffers a sudden heart attack and collapses. A doctor is summoned, but too late: the hypnotist is dead. The crowd can do nothing but stare up at the young man who continues to float "Up, up, until he was level with the top of the carnival tent, until he reached the height of the tallest trees—until he passed the trees and moved on into the soft moonlit sky of early October." (*Nine Horrors*, p. 40)

"On the Elevator" is a more traditional horror piece, right down to its unabashedly Gothic opening: "The storm had been building up far out at sea since early morning; by evening the full fury of it broke against the beach fronts. Mountainous gray waves rushed up the slopes of sand, washed across the boardwalks and churned into streets which paralleled the shore." (*Nine Horrors*, p. 62)

The storm causes the sea to wash up a very unwelcome visitor, a figure in a shiny black raincoat. This figure is sparsely described: "He had an odd, limp, *collapsed* look." When the clerk at the Atlas hotel sees the figure get into the elevator he summons the police. They arrive, only to find the body of one of the hotel guests in the elevator, his throat slashed, his features unrecognizable. They also find the black raincoat, encrusted with seaweed and smelling of salt water, and muddy tracks leading outside. A doctor at the autopsy suggests that the dead man's wounds were made not by a weapon but by *"incredibly long and powerful fingernails."* (The italics are Brennan's). The story closes with a paragraph that echoes the ending of "The Upper Berth" in which the clerk, pressed for an explanation of events, replies:

"Well, if you ask me, chum, that murderin' thing in the black raincoat was something dead that came up out of the sea!"

"The Horror at Chilton Castle" is a *tour de force* of unrelieved horror set in England and dealing with a hellish being endowed with eternal life that demands a cannibalistic feast once every generation. Brennan weaves genuine Anglo-Irish history into his tale, and lets the horror build slowly, sustaining the mood and atmosphere so pervasively that one can almost feel the slime-covered stairs of Chilton Castle:

> The end of the passage brought us to more descending steps. We went down some fifteen and entered another tunnel which appeared to have been cut out of the solid rock on which the castle had been built. White crusted nitre clung to the walls. The reek of mold was intense. The icy air was fetid with some other odor which I found particularly repellent, though I could not name it." (*The Shapes of Midnight*, p.119)

As usual with Brennan, there are no tangled convolutions of plot, no neurotic characters cluttering up the landscape, and no attempt to explain things away by psychology, parapsychology or any other ploy. The horror is just what is seems to be. The narrator, scared out of his wits, escapes to America, and, in the time-honored tradition, announces his intention "to keep Chilton Castle and its permanent occupant at least an ocean away."

Many of Brennan's stories involve ghosts or apparitions that make frightening, unexpected appearances in old houses, hospital rooms, or even, as in "The Man in Gray Tweeds," on the highway. The ghost story—a difficult and demanding genre—presents formidable obstacles, but Brennan's often succeed because they are written with conviction, deliberately understated, and are often genuinely frightening. In "Who Was He?" the narrator, who might well be Brennan himself, is in the hospital recovering from a coronary attack when he is approached by a little man, evidently a hospital barber, dressed in a seedy thin alpaca jacket and carrying a "small, rather disreputable black bag." The narrator sends him away. That day a patient across the corridor dies of a heart attack after emitting a hair-raising scream. A couple days later the barber reappears; the narrator again dismisses him. Shortly afterward another patient, this time just two rooms away, succumbs. The narrator befriends a security guard who tells him both patients were found dead with a look of fear on their faces, and that a little man carrying a black bag was seen fleeing along the corridor. When the narrator identifies the little man as the hospital barber he is told he is mistaken: the real barber is totally different in appearance. Stranger still, the little man's black bag, found after his escape, was opened and found to contain only dirt—dirt, which proves, under closer examination, to have come from a cemetery.

This accomplished little ghost story is told with just the right amount of conviction. Brennan is very skilled in supplying details of his phantoms' appearances—the thin alpaca cloth jacket and scuffed black bag of the hospital barber, the gray tweed suit worn by the man on the highway, the shiny black rubber raincoat worn by the thing in the elevator—and these disquieting images tend to linger in the reader's mind.

"Canavan's Back Yard" is one of Brennan's most admired stories. In this the narrator, going to see his friend Canavan the antiquarian book dealer, looks into his back yard and experiences the full horror of Lovecraft's nightmare geometry in which the landscape is "all wrong." When Canavan himself disappears the narrator goes into the back yard to look for him, finds that he is lost as the landscape begins to change, and then encounters the book dealer, apparently insane, crouched on all fours, who comes bounding after him. The narrator barely escapes with his life, not to mention his sanity. Later returning to the same spot, he sees "that monstrous landscape subtly alter its dimensions and perspectives until I was staring toward a stretch of blowing brindle grass and rotted trees which ran for miles." Unwisely, Brennan explains away some of the horror of Canavan's back yard by telling us a witch had put a curse on the spot after being torn to pieces by wild dogs there, but it is easy enough to ignore this contrivance. What counts is the story's pervasive power and, of course, the nightmarish landscape.

"The Dump" is one of Brennan's few excursions into science fiction. Not surprisingly, since the author is a traditionalist in all things, the future he envisions is hellishly akin to George Orwell's 1984. In this world a rat-infested dump is the alternative to life in a state-controlled world of plastic prefab, tronicars, food capsules, entertaintime programs and permaplastic coffins. The heroine, not surprisingly, makes her decision to live at the dump with other fugitives from the state, where, despite the rats and sea gulls, "at least she felt alive." This is hardly Brennan at his best, but then science fiction is not his long suit.

"I'm Murdering Mr. Massington," originally published in *Esquire*, is a bizarre anecdote concerning the title character, who, having confided the salient details of his life to a sympathetic narrator, a sometime writer, seems reasonably confident his name will endure when the narrator writes up his account. Thus assured of literary immortality, he sits down in a rented hotel room and fires a bullet into his brain. This disturbing little vignette is all the more effective for the quiet, matter-of-fact way it is presented.

"The Vampire Bat" is an amusing trifle concerning a man who is losing his blood to the nocturnal visits of a vampire bat, but cannot discover how the bat is getting in. When he dies from the loss of blood it is discovered the bat has been inside all along, living in the man's huge straw hat.

"Disappearance" is the kind of rural tale Brennan does best. After Dan Mellmer disappears an investigation is undertaken, but turns up nothing. After ten years his brother Russell dies of a heart attack. When the police return to the Mellmer farm they find Dan's mummified skeleton inside the scarecrow standing outside, where it has stood for ten years. When the narrator suggests Dan might have died naturally the sheriff points to the back of the skull.

A segment of the bone a good three inches in diameter had been shattered with such force there was a ragged hole in the skull.

"Offhand I'd say an axe," Sheriff Kellington said. "Or maybe a sledge hammer. I guess we'll never know for sure."

Many of Brennan's stories are set in the mythical New England town of Juniper Hill. Like Lovecraft's Arkham or King's Castle Rock (or, for that matter, Faulkner's Yoknapatawpha County), this small patch of Americana has its dark side. So much evil is festering there, in fact, and so many strange things occurring, so many grisly murders and mysterious disappearances, it seems surprising the National Guard hasn't been sent in. Yet for all the horror that goes on there, Juniper Hill is an idealized portrait of the small, rural, homespun New England town Brennan knows so well, in which the citizens gather at the town square and spend their evenings in an easy chair on the veranda, sipping lemonade or perhaps sarsaparilla. This is Brennan country.

BIBLIOGRAPHY

Short Story Collections:

1. *Nine Horrors and a Dream*, Arkham House, 1958, Ballantine Books, 1962. Includes: "Slime," "Levitation," "The Calamander Chest," "Death in Peru," "On the Elevator," "The Green Parrot," "Canavan's Back Yard," "I'm Murdering Mr. Massington," "The Hunt," "The Mail for Juniper Hill."

2. *The Dark Returners*, Macabre House, 1959. Includes: "Disappearance," "Goodbye, Mr. Bliss," "The Corpse of Charlie Rull," "The Impulse to Kill," "The Pool," "Daisy Murdock," "The Fete in the Forest," "Curb Service," "The Pavilion."

3. *Scream at Midnight*, Macabre House, 1963. Includes "The Horror at Chilton Castle," "The Midnight Bus," "The Vampire Bat," "The Seventh Incantation," "Killer Cat," "The Dump," "The Tenants," "The Man Who Feared Masks," "The Visitor in the Vault," "In the Very Stones."

4. *Stories of Darkness and Dread*, Arkham House, 1973. Includes "City of the Seven Winds," "The Keeper of the Dust," "Zombique," "The Seventh Incantation," "Delivery of Erdmore Street," "The Way to the Attic," "Mr. Octbur," "Episode on Cain Street," "Killer Cat," "In the Very Stones," "The House at 1248," "Black Thing at Midnight," "Monton," "Apprehension," "The House on Hazel Street," "The Man in Gray Tweeds," "The North Knoll," "The Dump."

5. *The Casebook of Lucius Leffing*, Macabre House, 1973. Includes "The Haunted Housewife," "Apparition in the Sun," "In Death as in Life," "The Strange Case of Peddler Phelps," "The Mantzen Diamond Mystery," "Death Mask," "The Mystery of Myrrh Lane," "Whirlwind of Blood," "The Intangible Threat," "The Ransacked Room," "Death at Draleman's Pond," "Death of a Derelict," "The Walford Case," "The Enemy Unknown," "The Dismal Flats Murder," "Fingers of Steel," "The Case of the Uncut Corpse."

6. *The Chronicles of Lucius Leffing*, Donald M. Grant, 1977. Includes: "The Case of the Hertzell Inheritance," "The Case of the Mystified Vendor," "The Apple Orchard Murder Case," "Mem'ries," "The Murder of Mr. Matthews," "The Possible Suspects," "The Dead of Winder Apparition," "The Nightmare Face."

7. *The Shapes of Midnight*, Berkley, 1980. Includes "Diary of a Werewolf," "The Corpse of Charlie Rull," "Canavan's Back Yard," "The Pavilion," "House of Memory," "The Willow Platform," "Who Was He?" "Disappearance," "The Horror at Chilton Castle," "The Impulse to Kill," "The House on Hazel Street," "Slime."

THE GRIM IMPERATIVE OF MICHAEL SHEA
by Arthur Jean Cox

Michael Shea first came to notice in 1974 with the publication of a rather curious book, *The Quest for Simbilis*: curious, because it was a sequel to a book by another writer. It had the same hero (as I suppose Cugel the Clever may be called) as *The Eyes of the Overworld* by Jack Vance, and it continued the action of Vance's story. It was a very spirited and inventive book and yet completely derivative. In other words, it was very much a young man's book and a first book...and it seemed for some time as if it were going to be his only book: for the author was not heard from again for half a decade.

I mention *The Quest for Simbilis* only to establish the background of the writer we are discussing. It is not itself a work of horror; but "The Angel of Death," Shea's next published story and his first short work of fiction (*F&SF*, August 1979) has sufficiently strong elements of horror to bring it within the present jurisdiction. Fortunately, it is well worth our attention.

"The Angel of Death" is the self-awarded and self-dignifying title of a shabby derelict who prowls the streets of a large city at night and murders love-making couples in parked cars. He is obviously based on New York City's "Son of Sam" killer...and here is an invitation to the cheapest and crudest of effects if there ever was one; but the author, while not surrendering any part of the interest in his subject, lifts it above mere sensationalism by the skill of his treatment and by something that must be called, for want of a better word, compassion. The derelict's real name is, aptly enough, Engelmann. He keeps a diary—I might add: of course—and his entries are marvels. I am strongly tempted to copy them out here, simply for the pleasure of seeing them reproduced under my own hand (a species of plagiarism), but will resist. I used the word compassion above; but for the understanding shown by the entries and by our occasional access to Engelmann's thoughts, compassion, that humane virtue ("dogged, blind, idiot compassion...the child of fear," Engelmann calls it) is too limited a word. The reader finds himself in the presence of a sensibility that has a more conscious dignity and a higher sense of personal drama than he himself has. There is a glory here that makes him conscious of what he has given up in becoming the polite, reasonable and decent human being that he is. Engelmann is a criticism of the reader...or so the reader thinks for one reckless moment, until he notes the realities of the man's immediate situation: the mattress on the floor before the television set, the box beside it containing candy bars, potato chips, cheese-n-cracker packs and the carton of chocolate milk that Engelmann likes to drink warm; until he remembers the ugly brutal senseless crimes in the street; and decides that he has, after all, chosen the Better Way. But there is something else, something that even Engelmann finds a distinct drawback to his way of life: he persistently, obstinately, dreams of large devouring spiders. He wonders about this.

> Granted, such things squirmed eternally behind the veil of nightmare. But why should he plunge so often into them? Why should his thought so tirelessly seek the worst it could?

He comes up with an answer, one that confirms his sense of egotistic grandeur...but the questions still linger in the reader's mind, for they seem to implicate more than the questioner. There are cross-linkages reaching sideways to the story's creator, whose thought tirelessly—as we see, looking back from the vantage point of his later stories—seeks the worst it can. And they reach sideways too (don't they?) to the reader himself, to the "aficionado" of horror fiction.

One of the most striking features of Engelmann's journal is the revelation of his sly and secret sanity. He knows what he is doing and he knows exactly what the doctors will say of him; but he doesn't care. He looks forward complacently to his eventual apprehension and to his comfortable life as an insane person in a hospital and the "soul-upholstering drugs" he will be given there. But his future is not to be what he thinks it is. Unknown to him, another "Angel of Death" has entered the picture: a cosmic scholar, a shape-changer aptly named Serif, visiting this planet and Engelmann's city. He assumes human shape (that of the optimum male, every woman's fantasy) and begins a study of human mating habits. He meets an appealing girl, and...and what the story is moving towards, of course, is the moment when Serif is pursuing his investigations with the girl in a car parked in a quiet side-street and they are interrupted by Engelmann. *Coitus interruptus perpetuus*...or so Engelmann thinks.

There are currents in the story other than horror—some unexpected moments of laughter, for instance—and it even has what must be considered a happy ending. But, never mind: it's all right. The author retrieves it for horror by flashing back, after the ending, to the last moments of the pathetic Engelmann, when his nightmares come true and his heady glory is horribly deflated. For the visiting scholar has taken Engelmann's action and his devouring-spider fantasies (of which he is directly aware) as being part of the mating ritual and obliges him by consummating them. This is a story which, making due allowances for differences in scale, easily bears comparison with the more famous productions of Stephen King. It is written with a degree of authority that is doubly impressive when one considers that it is only the writer's second published work.

As far as I can tell, "The Angel of Death" attracted no attention; but Shea's next story did attract some attention and, in fact, was nominated for the the Hugo and Nebula awards. This was "The Autopsy," published as the lead story in the December 1980 *F&SF*.

There must be many stories fully as gruesome and horrifying as "The Autopsy," but the word that compellingly suggests itself as we read this one is the word "grim." It is a word that I will be using more than once in the next few pages, so perhaps I should try to say what it is I understand it to mean. "Grim" has less intensity of feeling than either "terror" or "horror," but it has more sinew. "Grim" is hard, unyielding, forbidding and unflinching. "Terror" causes us to flee and "horror" to cringe; but "grim" challenges us to stand and face it and so has (we note with some surprise) a moral element that the other two terms lack. All this is very pertinent to "The Autopsy," which is possibly the grimmest story ever offered to the public as entertainment. The editor was obviously conscious of this and a little nervous about its reception. "And so be warned," he said in his prefatory note, "that it is in some ways a grim and horrifying tale"; but he softened a little the off-putting effect of this with the promise that "it is ultimately a positive, even a touching story." He was right on both counts and certainly right in being a little nervous. It is conjecturable—anyway, I am tempted to conjecture—that the failure of "The Autopsy" to win either of the two prizes for which it was nominated is attributable to its grimness. To me it seems a classic of its kind.

The story tells how Dr. Carl Winters, a pathologist dying of cancer, arrives in a small mining town to perform a series of autopsies. The town has been the scene of some particularly gruesome murders, but his dissections are to be of the bodies of the victims of a mine explosion, the apparent murderer being one of them. His cutting up of the corpses is briskly and graphically described, by someone who seems to know something of the subject. What he uncovers is another traveling cosmic "scholar," a darker development of some potentialities inherent in the Serif of the first story. The scene in which the Traveler reveals itself to Dr. Winters is one that is not easily forgotten and what follows is oppressive in the extreme. The doctor finds himself on the threshold of a fate that is literally worse-than-death—no one, I think, would withhold that description from it. But he manages to snatch a victory of sorts from defeat; a victory far grimmer than many defeats, but nevertheless a victory.

Shea's next story must have been eagerly awaited by others besides myself. It proved to be a novella, "Polyphemus" (*F&SF*, August 1981), which the author had described to the editor as "straightforward science fiction." So it would seem. A group of scientists are exploring and appropriating an unfamiliar planet and are trapped, in a chilling scene, on an island in a lagoon by a huge creature inhabiting the water. They call their captor Polyphemus, after the one-eyed giant in the *Odyssey*, because it resembles, as they see it, a gigantic eye surrounded by swarming cilia—something that is beautifully rationalized. Their problem is to kill it, or failing that, to escape the island without its killing them. In short, if "The Autopsy" belongs to the same genre as John W. Campbell's "Who Goes There?" this story belongs to that which was a spinoff from the Campbell story and which was initiated by A.E. van Vogt's "Black Destroyer" and "Discord in Scarlet." In other words, "straightforward science fiction"; but I think it worth noting here for reasons that shall be made clear as we go along.

The mentioned van Vogt stories are not themselves works of horror, although there was an element of horror latent in them (as was made manifest by the movie, *Alien*); but Shea, in obedience to his own imperatives, brings this element to the fore. He emphasizes the emotional effect upon his actors: "moan of horror," "trance of horror" and even "rapture of horror." But the chief thrust of the story is in defiance of this swooning response and it gives the story its narrative power and a tone very unlike that of van Vogt. "Do not look away!" cries the chief character, as two women are seized and horribly eaten. "*Do not look away!*"—this might be set as an epigraph at the head of a collection of Shea's writings. "Do not look away! We've got to know it to kill it." Here, "grim" comes to grips with "horror." "Horror" encourages passivity, but "grim" calls to action, a call which the story answers as it pushes forward, manfully, into the heart of the horrible: that is to say, as the hero swims into the very maw of Polyphemus and victory is once again, as in "The Autopsy," and literally this time, snatched from the jaws of defeat. The hero's action seems to me very suggestive...of just what I shall shortly say. The story as a whole is not as powerful as "The Autopsy"—not many stories are—but it is nevertheless a very impressive performance.

Michael Shea's second book was published by DAW the following year. It has since won a World Fantasy Award. *Nifft the Lean* is a collection of four stories, two of which seem to have been written in obedience to his imperative to tirelessly seek the worst. Both are novellas. I will discuss here only the first of the two, the lead story, "Come Then, Mortal—We Shall Seek Her Soul."

Nifft the Lean is a vagabond thief, in a world somewhat like that of *The Dying Earth*. He and a companion are traversing the wastelands when they are approached by a woman who is born, rather messily but finally "nude and whole," from the ground. She has a commission for them. They are to bring down to her in Hell the man who had betrayed her in life. Their reward is to be a certain Wizard's key of unlimited though unspecified powers. The bulk of the story tells of the kidnapping of the unhappy man; of Nifft's wrestling with the Demon of Death, which gains them entry to the Afterworld; and of the journey of the three through the various regions of Hell to their goal, the woman Dallisem. It is an odyssey of horror—it seems to me that the phrase "to sup on horrors" must have been coined specifically for this story. But there is a kind of counterpoint, another interest developing along the way, touching their captive and fellow-traveler, Dallisem's betrayer, Defalk: a cowardly, mean, yet proud and remorseful man. I like very much what Shea has done with him in this story. The treatment of him, beginning with disgust and contempt—intimate, sympathetic and slightly sickening—and moving towards respect and liking is very right; the relenting towards him in the face of, in the midst of, so much horror and suffering is very right and comes as a relief to the reader. I think it the best thing in the story, and, I wouldn't add, the most imaginative. I would trade it myself for all the demons in Shea's Hell.

Nifft survives his ordeals and returns to the daylight world, though without his companions and without the Wizard's Key, which proved to be a mere lure and deception. But the satisfaction the reader feels at Nifft's escape is seriously qualified. It is, after all, merely a temporary reprieve. For the Hell described is where the people of Nifft's world go when they die. It is where *he* will go when he dies. There seems to be no alternative place (and with Shea one feels there couldn't be) and so there is no escape, not even in death—especially, not in death. One would think that this would always hang over Nifft rather heavily; and I myself couldn't shake the consciousness of it while reading the other stories in the volume: not even the strongly competing horrors of "The Fishing of the Demon Sea" could drive it completely from my mind. Now, if I (forgive me!) had written the story, I don't think I would have permitted the revelation that the Wizard's Key was a fraud. Why shouldn't it be something that would allow Nifft, at his own death, to escape the horrors he has already experienced and witnessed? Something that would enable him to achieve a more blessed state? Or, if that is asking too much, then why shouldn't it be something that would give him access to that one thing that would have to be counted, in such a world, as its greatest blessing: simple, permanent extinction? This hope, this priceless promise or real death, would permit Nifft to carry on his further adventures with a lighter heart—something that would surely be a great boon to a picaresque rogue. But here, no doubt, I have strayed from the path of criticism and am merely spinning out a fantasy of my own, parasitic upon Shea's achieved triumph. He himself would never violate so grossly the imperative to tirelessly seek the worst.

It is curious to consider Shea's relationship with the genre of horror fiction. Almost everything he has written so far is shot through with dread and menace, is darkly stained and sometimes congealed with the gruesome and the grotesque (as in that curdled mixture of the hilarious and the horrific, "That Frog," in the April 1982 *F&SF*); and yet he has written only one conventional—or, if you prefer, traditional—horror story, "The Horror on the #33," in the August 1982 *F&SF*. This may be because his real allegiance, as I have already hinted, is not to horror but to the grim. As we read, or re-read, his stories in sequence we become aware that what he seeks is not so much, or not only, the emotion of fear but that of courage. Horror is indispensable, but it is only half the story; the other half is the defiance of horror. In story after story, we see him go down, down...down into an oppressive and claustrophobic nightmare of life-in-death (as in "The Autopsy"), down into the maw of Polyphemus, down into the Demon Sea and down into Hell itself. Again and again, he plunges resolutely into them, as if to test himself against them: as if nothing but the most truly horrible could satisfy him, as if only it could be really respected, as if only it were unimpeachably authentic. My own suspicion is that he seeks the worst there is in scorn of the Specious Good, that he has a strongly held though perhaps unspoken conviction that any conception of happiness that has not made itself acquainted with the worst there is, that lives in ignorance of suffering, despair and death, is no true happiness but a kind of fool's paradise. If this suspicion is right, then his stubborn adherence to that grim imperative to tirelessly seek the worst can be seen as ultimately in the service of health and happiness.

But, regardless of whether it is right or not, we can still conclude, we can only conclude, that he has written some marvelous stories. Two or three of them—certainly, "The Angel of Death" and "The Autopsy"—are masterpieces of their kind, and two or three others are almost of their company. This is a remarkable showing when one considers how recently he appeared on the scene and how few stories he has had published: only ten at the time of this writing. I am filled with envy as I read them and with a growing admiration for a talent that is at once so robust and so delicate. Michael Shea is as yet a comparatively young man, and—laying aside for a moment the Grim Imperative and seeking instead, and wishing instead, only for the best there is—we can feel reasonably confident that he has decades of writing life ahead of him. It is a pleasure to hail such a talent near the beginning of so promising a career.

SARDONIC FANTASISTES: JOHN COLLIER
by Ben P. Indick

An unusually omnivorous orchid swallows a cat, a maiden aunt and a careless young man. A love potion works *too* well. A man is loved by a silent yet eloquent chimpanzee who dreams of wedding him. A mutually adoring couple discovers the unfortunate consequences of over-insurance. They are but a few of the inhabitants of the world of John Collier, who once wrote: "Man is reflected in his consciousness, and has noted that the image is largely dependent on the darker side of the pain-pleasure principle for its clarity."[1] It was a philosophy which would inspire his sardonic vision of humanity.

For those whose taste delights in a fictional rapier thrust, sharp, clean, unbloodied, there is no practitioner superior to Collier, and few indeed can pack an equivalent wallop into several well-chosen words. In "The Chaser" two words suffice. The secret of a murder mystery is revealed in another pair of words in "The Touch of Nutmeg Makes It," and, likewise, the final crushing irony in "Green Thoughts" requires no more than two words. This is truly literary economy. Yet, his beautifully proportioned language is his surest tool, the product perhaps of his early years writing poetry.

A naturally reclusive man, Collier lived until his death in 1980 in England as a gentleman farmer. Famed as novelist, screenwriter, and especially for his short stories, he avoided biographers and even *Who's Who*. There is a biography on the Penguin reprint of his novel *Defy the Foul Fiend*, so elegantly phrased that we may accept it as his own writing. He was born in 1901 and began writing poetry at 18. "He subsisted at this time" it states, "on the generosity of an indulgent father, and thus developed an addiction to games of chance, conversation in cafes, and visits to picture galleries."[2] His poetry was published in magazines and in book form; tightly written, enigmatic and imagistic, it impressed him less than the poetry of Edith Sitwell and the poetic prose of James Joyce. In 1930 he began writing prose. His first effort was a novel, *His Monkey Wife*, followed by a second, *Tom's A-Cold* (published in America as *Full Circle*), and then, in 1934, *Defy the Foul Fiend*. At the same time he was writing the short stories which would give him fame. In 1936 he collaborated on his first screenplay, which would be followed by at least seven others.[3]

The quality most popularly associated with Collier is that which has inspired this series: the sardonic. In this interpretation, it is more than satire. It is a look at Man as an essentially comic, even foolish creature, given to actions seemingly inevitable yet irrelevant to his own well-being, and usually the result of avarice, greed and selfishness. The reader acquainted with the author will have no delusions about what he may expect and would be disappointed were it anything else. The flavor is in Collier's style, a spareness and yet a sparkling felicity with words, so that we recognize the universality of the fallibilities of his characters; because he so often employs an ironic humor, we can laugh at them and at ourselves. It is thus less the nature of the climax itself than the manner in which it is achieved which makes the reading so rewarding.

One may discern several categories which stand out in his writing, primarily in the short fiction but to varying degrees in his novels as well:

1. Demonology, invariably light and bantering in tone.
2. Outright ghost stories, among the few of his non-humorous pieces.
3. Guignol, the sense of true horror, although ironic.
4. The relationship of men and women, usually inamicable, and initially anti-feminine.[4]

One must assume that imps, demons, succubi and even a few angels were among John Collier's favorite acquaintances, for they appear in so many stories. "Fallen Star," "Pictures in the Fire," "The Devil, George, and Rosie," "Hell Hath No Fury," "Thus I Refute Beelzy" are but a few. It is not uncommon for the hero to summon a demon for the purpose of making a pact with the devil. Happily, the hero does not always suffer from such a rash action; indeed, he rarely does. In "Pictures in the Fire" the demon neglects to take up an option in the negotiated contract, and the hero escapes. In "The Devil, George, and Rosie" an incorrigibly good woman, who even makes a virtue of being seduced, forces Satan to chase her and her young man from Hades.

There are variations on Demonry as well. In "The Possession of Angela Bradshaw" the demon, who has temporarily possessed the comely young woman's body, turns out to be a modern poet, a comment in itself. In "Thus I Refute Beelzy" the demon is never seen at all until the frightening proof of his intangible existence is irrefutably proven.

Collier's lifelong interest in Satan and his significance eventually resulted in a serious work, a screenplay based directly upon Milton's epic poem *Paradise Lost*. In one sense this play may be seen as a logical and final exposition of the opposing elements within humankind's psyche, not in the religious sense, but in a more contemporary sense of Individualism.

Collier's inquisitive eye usually prefers humorous irony, but he has written several genuine ghost stories. "Are You Too Late or Was I Too Early?" is the flippant title for a Maupassantesque tale of a man who lives alone in this thoughts. One may sense the mood of this piece in such a line as "My fingers are horribly blistered by the cigarettes that burn down between them while still I walk in the company of women with the heads of cats." In "The Lady On the Grey" a curious revenge is exacted on the descendants of the English who had exploited the Irish in Ireland. "Bird of Prey" is a harrowing account of jealousy, written around a pet parrot. In the end, when the distraught husband has killed the innocent wife and then himself, "the parrot, or whatever it was, sailing down, seized what came out of his ruined mouth and wheeled back toward the window, and was soon far away, visible for the moment only as it swept on broader wings past the new-risen moon." There is irony in these stories, but they are not playful.

Generally, when Collier employs Guignol, with its attendant murder and horror, he leavens it with ironic humor at the expense of some unfortunate if deserving wretch (and sometimes some undeserving ones as well). Such a denouement may include dismay, agony and even dismemberment; the humor is in the narrative style which tells us that the fate was, after all, well-earned, a mock lesson and a wry comment on the workings of Fate. The doctor in "Back For Christmas" who has laboriously chopped his annoying wife into pieces and buried her in neat parcels in the cellar leaves home for a presumed vacation, only to learn that his late wife had arranged to have a new cellar built in his absence. In "Green Thoughts" a horticulturist is literally absorbed, physically, by his unusual new orchid. When his avaricious nephew sees his uncle's face within the flower, and then discovers that the uncle's intention had been to cut him from his will, he snatches up a scissors...

Another nephew is less fortunate in "Another American Tragedy." When he learns that his uncle is removing his name from the will, he has all his own teeth removed, slips his dying uncle from his deathbed and takes the old man's place there. He summons the lawyer to write a new will, reinstating himself. Most regrettably for his ambition, an equally avaricious physician *already* in the will, arrives first, and decides that his dying patient's newly found avanacular devotion indicates a "mental derangement." He thereupon proceeds to open up the nephew's interior, ludicrously, and to the distress of the latter, permanently. This burlesque Guignol, told in sophisticated and satiric manner, is perhaps the most widely attributed quality of the author.

His Guignol, however, on occasion, retains the verve and shock without the relieving laughter, most classically in "The Touch of Nutmeg Makes It." A story of a particularly repellent murder, the work of an apparent madman, it is all the more peculiar that a sensitive, mild-mannered man has been accused of so heinous a crime. It is logical that no jury could accept him as a murderer, and he is acquitted; however, a subsequent trivial incident demonstrates more about the man than any amount of circumstantial evidence might. In "Special Delivery," a man falls in love with a department store mannequin; there is no humor as the story follows his stealing the doll to his eventual death at the hands of hooligans. Yet there is a disquieting fascination in his hopeless love, with its terrible fate as he is kicked to death and thrown with the mannequin into a chalk pit. "His head lay limp on her neck; her stiff arm was arched over him. In the autumn, when the overhang crumbled down on them, it pressed him close to her forever."

The love of a man for a doll is a clue to Collier's attitude toward the male/female relationship. He had begun writing his novels when the *new woman* was flexing a newfound muscle. To Collier it must have seemed a false citified sophistication at odds with the natural manly quality of rural, simple life. His first novel explicated upon it with satire. *His Monkey Wife*, subtitled "Married to a Chimp" is an intended double entendre.

The book describes what Collier saw as the young woman of the day, unwilling to enter into an honest and firm relationship with a man, desirous of the surface pleasures of money and society. It is also a riotous parody wherein an Englishman, teaching in Africa, becomes the love-object of his pet chimp, Emily. When he returns to England, he brings Emily along to become the maid of Amy, his fiancee. He is unaware that Emily, desirous only for his well-being, has learned to read English and to type. Emily quickly realizes that Amy is a selfish woman who cannot give her beloved Mr. Fatigay true love. After many delays which Amy has caused, a marriage date is set; however, on that occasion, for her master's good, Emily seizes the bridal gown and forces Amy to be the bridesmaid. Mr. Fatigay and Emily are betrothed, but when he removes the veil, he is shocked. Turning to the clergyman, he cries out "Hi sir! Hi sir! You have married me to a chimp!"

Amy, making capital of a bad situation, pretends she had forced the chimp to take her place, to avoid a foolish marriage, and resumes her society life. Mr. Fatigay goes to seed, but is finally saved by the resourceful Emily, and, in a newly found success, even gives Amy her comeuppance. Mr. Fatigay returns with Emily to Africa to live as man and wife. To the newspapermen he says: "It is true my wife is not a woman...but though I firmly believe that there is no chimp like my Emily, I can heartily recommend my fellow men to seek their life's pal...among the females of her modest race. Behind every great man there may indeed be a woman, and neath every performing flea a hot plate, but beside the only happy man I know of—there is a chimp."

In his non-fantasy novel, *Defy the Foul Fiend*, Collier touches more realistically on the same theme. His bastard hero, something of a modern Tom Jones, flees from an embarrassing incident involving the voluptuous wife of his employer to the rural, rustic home of his uncle. The simple honesty of the life there is in clear distinction to the exciting but brittle and false life of city society. When he falls in love, and the love is reciprocated, accident prevents their marriage; later, as it becomes possible, it is too late. The type of life to which each has become accustomed is irreconcilable. The marriage fails. The author, in a lyrical passage about Love and its durability, writes: "Our young couple lived happily ever after, for what is *ever* but eternity, and the year that followed was an eternal year...never to be forgotten...and never to be repeated." The hero is not disgruntled; he could have loved her still, but his life on the estate, which he has now inherited, is not to his dislike either.

In his short fiction, the ladies do not always lack their triumph, as if to indicate that they are not invariably to blame; nevertheless it is usually the husband, annoyed by a wife like that in "Back for Christmas" who initiates the action. Another henpecked husband, in "Three Bears Cottage" plans to kill his wife with a deadly mushroom. In an uncharacteristic generosity, she upsets his plans by serving him the tidbit instead of keeping it for herself, her usual wont. And indeed, thereupon makes interesting new plans for herself involving a handsome young woodcutter. In "Mary," a woman must compete for the love of her new husband with his pet performing pig; the intuitive reader may guess the ultimate disposition of this pig. In "The Frog Prince," the woman the hero had planned to jilt in favor of an attractive but wealthier one married that heiress herself! An ineffectual writer in "Collaboration," strong in style but weak in plot, collaborates with a writer weak in style but strong in plot. His wife, who has put up with all his pretensions, learns to collaborate herself, and produces in time an interesting set of siblings. "Sleeping Beauty" concerns a woman of great beauty who is aroused from her sideshow status as an endless sleeper by a man hopelessly in love with her. Unfortunately, she proves to be a mean-minded and petty individual and causes him to lose his fortune. Happily, he regains his fortune and her silent beauty by a simple expedient.

If Collier had been less than chivalric toward women in his prior work, his attitude changed when, in 1973, he adapted *Paradise Lost* as a screenplay, subtitling it "For the cinema of the mind" in the realization it bore small chance for actual filming. In his foreword, he insists that Eve is his heroine, rather than being a weak, near-villain as in Scripture. Adam, oafish in his willing and fearful subjugation to God, is only made into a genuinely individualistic self by Eve's act,

125

"the deed," Collier writes, "which is that story's *raison d'etre*." It is she who actually teaches the need for love and mutuality to Adam. The mordant wit and humor of his earlier work is absent here, but it is a powerful and colorful story, quite filmable were any producer so inclined.

Quite apart from the mainstream of his writing is Collier's second novel, *Tom's A-Cold*. It is a story of the ruined world of 1995, with people huddled into small rural groups trying to survive in the rubble-heaps of the old world. The men outnumber the women, and it is not uncommon for one group to raid another to seize females. In his foreword, the author insists it is not a "sociological" tale, but it is a bitter evocation of a painful future, brought on by the unchanging nature of man. The language varies from abrupt and short speech and prose to Shakespearean cadences, helping to make the book unique in his canon. A Collier admirer will search in vain here for the satire and irony of his novels, or the brittle and brilliant malice of his short stories.

In the end, we remember most pleasurably Collier as observer and dazzling wordsmith. "He at once shot out of his chair, and began to leap, stagger, spin, curve, gyrate, look and flounder all over the room" is his description of the antics of the poisoned husband in "Three Bears Cottage." When the bemused Willoughby of *Defy the Foul Fiend* tells his new love "You have the soul of a little girl in the body of a courtesan," Collier mocks his hero's juvenile attempt at sophistication by noting: "She was not in the least offended by the vile bad taste of this remark, nor by its triteness."

He expressed his own philosophy well in 1933: "As a writer, my position is a difficult one. I cannot see much good in the world, nor much likelihood of good. There seems to be a definite bias in human nature towards ill, towards the immediate convenience, the vulgar, the cheap...I cannot therefore believe very enthusiastically in myself or my fellow man...You might think from the foregoing that I must be the most miserable man alive; on the contrary, I know no one as happy."[6]

It is because John Collier can laugh at the dark side of humankind that he can be "happy." In sharing his laughter, we share in his understanding.

NOTES

1. From "The Apology," his Introduction to his book of poems, *Gemini*, 1931.
2. Penguin Books edition of Collier's *Defy the Foul Fiend*, 1948.
3. Collier's first screenplay was "Sylvia Scarlett," with Katherine Hepburn and Cary Grant. He collaborated on *Elephant Boy*, then wrote *Her Cardboard Lover, Deception, Roseanna McCoy* (about a

Kentucky mountaineer feud, no less!), part of the omnibus *Story of Three Loves, I Am A Camera* and *The War Lord*. In his Foreword to *The John Collier Reader*, 1972, Anthony Burgess indicates that Collier is responsible for *The African Queen*; however, so far as I have been able to determine, this is strictly the work of John Agee and John Huston, adapted from the novel by C.S. Forester. According to *Presenting Moonshine*, a fanzine devoted to Collier, he also did a number of TV scripts as well, including the Alfred Hitchcock series.

4. Collier's early attitude toward the fair sex may be gleaned from lines in his poem "Three Men in One Room," printed in *Gemini*:
> "And so with women, since some little care
> Of pretty custom causes them forbear
> Flesh teeth upon our carcases, they find
> Means to devour the spirit and the mind."

5. Quoted from John Gawsworth's *Ten Contemporaries, Second Series*, as quoted in *Presenting Moonshine* No. 7.

BIBLIOGRAPHY

His Monkey Wife. Peter Davies, London, 1930.

No Traveller Returns. White Owl Press, 1931.

Tom's A-Cold. MacMillan, 1933. (American title: *Full Circle*) D. Appleton, New York, 1933.

The Devil and All. Nonesuch Press, 1934.

Presenting Moonshine. Macmillan, London, 1941.

A Touch of Nutmeg, and More Unlikely Stories. Press of the Readers Club, New York, 1943.

Fancies and Goodnights. Doubleday, New York, 1951.

Pictures in the Fire. Rupert Hart-Davis, London, 1958.

The John Collier Reader. Knopf, New York, 1972.

HISTORY AS HORROR:
CHELSEA QUINN YARBRO
by Gil Fitzgerald

Many contemporary horror novels have incorporated fragments of ancient folklore into their plotlines, and in most of them the supernatural element is the basis for all the chills and thrills. In *'Salem's Lot*, a prosperous New England village is invaded by a vampire and reduced to a ghost town inhabited by the undead. *The Wolfen* presents a tribe of eerily intelligent superwolves, co-existing with mankind throughout the ages and the basis of the werewolf legends, running loose in New York City and picking off bums. *Pet Sematary* brings the dead back to life—but terribly changed. In *The Hour of the Oxrun Dead* a librarian discovers that the books on mainstream religion are vanishing from the library shelves and being replaced by tomes on Satanism—because the town's leading citizens are devil-worshipers. Vampires, werewolves, zombies, Satanists—all the stuff of nightmares.

But must all creatures of the night be evil by nature? What happens if the supernatural creature is the hero of the book? Where does the horror come from?

Chelsea Quinn Yarbro has answered these questions in her brilliant series of novels about the Count de Saint Germain. She carefully examined the vampire mythos in order to discover its key elements, and decided there was no intrinsic reason for vampires to be evil. After all, what is it that vampires actually do? They are impervious to most forms of death, though drowning, severing of the spinal cord, and burning will kill them. They are able to confer this conditional immortality upon others through an act which seems to give pleasure to both vampire and victim alike. Of course, the eroticism in the blood-kiss would have been enough to convince Puritans and Victorians of the vampire's demonic origins—but most people today do not consider sex between consenting adults evil. Of course, if they change the victim without permission it would be akin to rape. But a rapist vampire would make himself conspicuous, and would tend to have a short life span. Yarbro's hero, the Count de Saint Germain, is the quintessence of the successful vampire.

Saint Germain is based on the notorious 18th-century alchemist-magician who caused such a stir at the French court. This mysterious gentleman was known to speak many languages, never ate or drank in public, always dressed in black and white, and for forty years maintained the appearance of an urbane and handsome 42. A gifted musician and a lover of women, he also possessed great wealth, and his origins were never discovered. Originally Yarbro planned to use Saint Germain as a minor background character in an historical vampire novel, but she realized there was no need to create a vampire when the Count possessed so many of the archetypal attributes. So in *Hotel Transylvania*, a dark-eyed man strode down a dark Parisian alley to a squalid taproom, and Francois Ragoczy, Count de Saint Germain, made his entrance into literary history.

Perhaps the most important difference between the Count and the other vampires is that he is both the hero and the protagonist of the series. He *is* the good guy, as well as the central character. It is his compassion and wisdom, as well as his wit and intelligence, which dominate the books, frequently in opposition to the self-centered and cruel normal humans. When the series opens, he is already two thousand years old, with a past cloaked in mystery, though it is Dacian earth he claims as his native soil—placing him as originating in the area which will someday be called Transylvania. He has had centuries in which to develop his sensitivity and his value system, and it is these, rather than his supernatural abilities, which set him apart from the mass of humanity. Taking the long view has wrought changes upon him, and he does not look at life in the same way as ordinary mortals. He has lived with human greed and cruelty for too long to be shocked by it, but he is still sickened and angered. If humanity is defined as empathy, the Count has more than most of us.

But if the vampire is the hero, where does the horror come from? These books are, after all, billed as historical horror novels. In most vampire novels, the vampire provides the horror, simply by existing.

Yarbro solved her problem by placing her vampire in opposition to mortal villains. It is human vices which create the horror, and thus give impetus to the plot, not vampirism. The Count's compassion and empathy are contrasted with ordinary human lust, greed, hunger for power, and fanaticism. At first glance these garden variety sins might seem tame, but Yarbro forces us to see how truly terrible human beings can be. She makes us look at the dark possibilities within ourselves, and she allows us the distancing of history to make it bearable.

To many, history is an impersonal study, dry as old bones, a collection of facts. Yarbro has steeped herself in the daily life of the times she has chosen. She knows what people ate for breakfast as well as at banquets, what they wore around the house as well as in formal portraits. This attention to detail pays off in vividly realized three-dimensional characters who embody their time and place. The reader

129

cares about these characters, and when historical forces create a situation which places them in danger, history becomes real.

The decadence of Rome is well-known to anyone who ever watched an episode of *I, Claudius*, but the in-fighting in the imperial family can seem like a game of Monopoly played for very high stakes. Characters are killed off with the same regularity as the victims in the splatter film—and we care even less, because the noble Romans were such an unpleasant lot. It is easy to forget that the power plays took their toll on many innocent bystanders, the real victims. In *Blood Games*, this cut-throat ambition is personified by Justus Silius, an aristocrat who aspires to the purple. As debauched as any of Nero's relatives, he is only sexually aroused when he watches his lovely young wife Olivia raped by gladiators. After sending her father and brothers to their deaths by implicating them in a plot against the emperor, he then blackmails her into staying with him by threatening her mother and sister. It is no wonder that Olivia seeks comfort in the arms of Saint Germain.

But Justus is not finished. When he sees a chance to ally himself with the Flavians, the family of Vespasian, he decides to rid himself of Olivia. However, he has already divorced one wife (after driving her mad) and he does not want the scandal of a second divorce. Instead, he fakes a poisoning, and the blame falls on Olivia, who is sentenced to be walled up alive in a tomb.

Justus' cruelty is in stark contrast to the Count's concern for all who are connected with him. He makes an enemy of the Master of the Bestiarii by not allowing his female charioteer (and lover) Tishtry to be beaten for refusing an order which would have crippled her team. He refuses to sell another slave, Kozrozd, to the Persians, who need him for political reasons since he is the only son of a rebellious prince. He helps Olivia who has known nothing but abuse at the hands of her husband, to discover joy—and earns Justus' enmity. Eventually these kindnesses cost him Tishtry, and Autehoutep, his Egyptian steward, and he is forced to watch helplessly, as they are torn to pieces in the arena for the pleasure of a bloodthirsty crowd. Not long after, he himself is in a flooded arena, stripped of his earth-soled boots, naked to the painful rays of the sun—the price he must pay for having loved Olivia.

Path of the Eclipse pits the Count against the Chinese antipathy toward foreigners, Mongol hordes, and a beautiful devotee of Kali. Forced to leave his comfortable home and abandon the treasures he has collected over a long lifetime, Saint Germain agrees to aid a proud young woman warlord in her attempt to protect her holdings against the Mongol invaders. T'en Chih Yuh becomes his lover, and she holds the promise of filling the emptiness he has felt since he fled Europe and the superstition of the Dark Ages which have robbed him of old loves and old friends. When she is killed during a particularly bloody battle, Saint Germain searches the battlefield, picking his way past pyramids of severed limbs and heads, until he finds her body so that he can give her a proper burial. Crossing the Himalayas, he comes to India where he is sent to stay with the middle-aged, intellectual sister of the local rajah. Padmiri's quiet intelligence helps to heal him, but he runs afoul of the ruler's lovely, blood-mad daughter, who has her father murdered and assumes the throne. Having recognized Saint Germain as a drinker of blood, she identifies him with Shiva and desires him as partner in her worship of Shiva's consort, Kali. A weaker novel than *Blood Games* because it lacks a strong plot connecting the episodes, the book still offers some strong scenes, particularly the bloody battlefield with its grisly pyramid.

The Palace is set in Renaissance Florence, the city of Lorenzo de Medici, Il Magnifico, a much sunnier place. It is the time of Botticelli and Michaelangelo, when beauty and learning were revered. Even Lorenzo, that consummate financier and politician, was a talented poet. It is his presence, brilliant as the gold brocade worn by the aristocrats, which dominates the first half of the book, and it is impossible not to care when a stricken Saint Germain realizes his friend is dying (of leukemia, it would seem) and he is powerless to save him. All he can do is promise to befriend Lorenzo's mistress and librarian, the cool, blonde Demetrice, who becomes Saint Germain's student in alchemy. Yet even in this wonderful setting, there is a dark side. The Catholic Church is ruled by a corrupt clergy, presided over by a Borgia pope who is more interested in advancing the interests of his bastard children than in preserving Christianity. In response to this decadence, a reformer comes forth, the Dominican preacher, Savanarola. At first only concerned with the corruption in the Church, like some fifteenth-century Jerry Falwell, he soon preaches against all worldly pleasures, condemning Lorenzo and those who surround him. Saint Germain is forced to flee, but returns, disguised as his own nephew, to rescue Demetrice who has been taken as a heretic.

Yarbro's portrayal of a city ruled by a fanatic is chilling. Botticelli wonders why his Christian paintings are lifeless while his pagan scenes burst with vitality. As Saint Germain watches, wearing monk's robes, Botticelli must place his own paintings in the fire as a symbol of his renunciation of the world. Can an artist imagine a more terrible fate than to be forced to destroy his own works? Estasia, Botticelli's hysterical cousin, has turned from her preoccupation with sensuality to the ultimate high of mysticism, but her ecstasies are tinged with madness and lust turned inward. The fires of the auto da fe burn brightly, and the final rescue of a dead Demetrice from the flames is a study in suspense.

By the time of *Hotel Transylvania*, set in 18th century France, the Count is again alone. Olivia has died the real death, crushed in a building collapse, and Demetrice, unable to adjust to her new existence as a vampire, has long since left him. He is lonely, drawing his sustenance during midnight visits to unloved wives who remember it as an erotic dream. These sad ladies are the product of their age, when the marriage of convenience was a way of life, and unfaithful, debt-ridden or homosexual husbands were burdens to be borne. It is a world of gleaming satins and rich laces, of glittering jewels and powdered hair, banquets and balls and masques—but there is rot beneath the gilden veneer, a rot which will, in a few decades, cause the barbarity of the French Revolution. The Count is all too aware of the decay, and this increases his own malaise.

Then, at a ball, he meets Madelaine de Montalia. Beautiful, witty, educated, charming—she is everything he has ever sought in a woman. More than that, she recognizes him as a vampire, and is intrigued rather than frightened. It is she who seduces him. For the first time in all those thousands of years Saint Germain knows complete love and acceptance. But the same rot that will bring down the French throne threatens Madelaine whose father had promised his first-born child to a Satanic cult. The leader, Saint Sebastien, plans to sacrifice Madelaine in a Black Mass, and it is up to the Count to save her from her fate.

The final book in the quintet is *Tempting Fate*, an apt description of the Count's mood as he watches the world attempt to destroy itself once again. Escaping from a Bolshevik prison, he rescues an orphaned girl and flees to Germany. In France, Madelaine is dealing with the effects of World War I, and falling in love with a charming American war correspondent. In the lull between the two wars, Saint Germain raises his adopted daughter, Laisha, who grows into a lovely and gifted teenager, and becomes involved with a German woman, wife of a paralyzed war hero. Gudrun's brother, Maximillien, unfortunately comes onto the scene, bringing with him his associates in the newly formed Nazi party. The unrest grows, and the hatred for foreigners reaches a fever pitch, causing the death of 16-year-old Laisha at the hands of a mob. The Count, driven to madness, goes after her killers and rips them limb from limb. World War II looms on the horizon as the book ends.

Yarbro's stark, restrained style creates scenes that linger long after the book is finished. The row of crucified prisoners set ablaze as torches to light an imperial banquet, the arena execution of Tishtry and Autehoutep, and Saint Germain's agony at their death. The ghastly pyramids of human limbs and heads left by the Mongols after a battle. The bonfire into which Botticelli must cast his paintings, the children of his soul, and the burning of the heretics. The Black Mass at which La Cressie is repeatedly raped while her uncaring husband watches. The description of soldiers marching in mud to the hip, and sinking down, drowning, only to be found weeks later when a trench is dry. Laisha, young and lovely and gifted, shot by a fanatic mob.

This is the real horror, not the vampirism of Saint Germain, and no supernatural creature can equal the darkness of our own souls.

Yet there is another theme running through the series, and that is the essential loneliness of a creature like Saint Germain. He is the eternal outsider, unable to linger long in one place for fear that someone will notice that he does not age. Humans he loves grow old and ill and die, and he is forced to watch helplessly, as he must with Lorenzo. The world goes mad around him, and as he tells Madelaine, sometimes he has gone mad with it as he did in Wallachia (presumably as Vlad Tepes, the historical Dracula). He has loved many women—but all have returned his love guardedly. Olivia loved him out of need; if she had not married a sadist, she would never have turned to Saint Germain. Tishtry enjoyed his attentions but preferred a more ordinary lover who could give her children. T'en Chih might have filled the emptiness in his life, but she was slain by the Mongols before he could change her to a vampire. Demetrice's heart belonged only to Lorenzo, and she accepted Saint Germain's kisses only out of despair and fear. It was not until Madelaine that a woman loved him whole-heartedly and freely, choosing him in the full knowledge of his nature, even longing to share it.

Since the Count's search for a partner to share his immortality (though not his bed, since one vampire cannot bite another), there is an aura of restrained eroticism about the books. Without resorting to four-letter words or purple prose, Yarbro conveys the sensuality of a night spent in Saint Germain's arms. She never tells us exactly what the Count does with his small, beautiful hands, but it is obviously delightful and few women readers would mind a lover like Saint Germain. The passion in these scenes is all the more effective because it is muted.

It is the combination of these themes—the dark side of the human soul and the loneliness of the immortal vampire who must witness the effects of that darkness, century after century—which gives the Saint Germain novels their strength. Yarbro reveals, through the rich tapestry of history, the depths to which man can sink, and the heights to which he aspires. If there is horror in history, there is also heroism and love. She shows us despair and decadence, but she also gives us hope, for men and women like Olivia and Madelaine, Lorenzo and Botticelli, Petronius and James Tree endure in spite of the turmoil surrounding them. Saint Germain, immortal and ever compassionate, is a testimony to the survival of hope.

BIBLIOGRAPHY

Hotel Transylvania. St. Martin's Press, 1978.
The Palace. St. Martin's Press, 1978.
Blood Games. St. Martin's Press, 1980.
Path of the Eclipse. St. Martin's Press, 1981.
Tempting Fate. St. Martin's Press, 1982.

QUIETLY SOARING: PETER TREMAYNE
by Christina Kiplinger

It began with *The Hound of Frankenstein*, in London, 1977. It progressed with *Dracula Unborn* and *The Vengeance of She*. Now, with a total of fourteen books to his credit, Peter Tremayne's creative talent is being introduced and accepted more and more by the American public.

As more readers delve into the work of Tremayne, one question looms above the descriptive prose of this new name. *Who* is Peter Tremayne?

Peter Tremayne was born across the hills of Trewern Round in England, in 1977. He was born of an idea. An idea about incorporating historical facts into salable fantasy fiction.

Peter Berresford Ellis, father of the idea, was living in London when he decided to take a chance with fantasy. Born March 10, 1943, Ellis had held a variety of jobs before succumbing to the fulltime career of writing. Dishwasher, rifle attendant, and bus conductor were only a few of the jobs Ellis had held, but whether the influence came from his father, a journalist, or his life as the youngest son in a large family, Ellis knew that he wanted to write as a career. In 1968, after a variety of jobs in the field of writing, Ellis threw his hat into the literary ring with *Wales—A Nation Again*. Historical, factual books became Ellis's forté. By 1977, Ellis was well established as a writer and he found himself entertaining thoughts of writing about vampires, quests and zombies. Having written at least one nonfiction book a year from 1968-1977, Ellis decided that it was time to try fantasy.

"People generally like to stereotype an author..." says Ellis about taking on a pseudonym, "so I had to choose a pseudonym for my fantasy work."

The first Tremayne title was published in London (1977). *The Hound of Frankenstein* was closely followed by *Dracula Unborn* (London, 1977). With *Dracula Unborn*, readers saw the romantic gentle side of Tremayne that would become characteristic of his work. They also saw a horrific pen.

...Her face, which before had been beautiful and wanton, was now distorted by pain and wild hatred. Her teeth, which somehow seemed longer than they should be, bit feverishly at her lips until the blood was trickling from them. And her eyes, which had been mischievous and infinitely seductive, were now wild and demented, hypnotized by the mark of the cross that was burnt on her bosom. (p.149, Dell edition)

Bloodright is the title of the U.S.A. edition of *Dracula Unborn.* Because of the popularity of *Dracula Unborn*, Tremayne was asked to develop the idea into a trilogy of novels. Before and during the process of writing the two remaining books, Tremayne came out with *Masters of Terror: William Hope Hodgson* (London, 1977), *The Vengeance of She* (London, 1978), *The Ants* (London, 1979), *Irish Masters of Fantasy* (Dublin, 1979), *The Curse of Loch Ness* (London, 1979) and *The Fires of Lan Kern* (London, 1980). *The Revenge of Dracula* (London, 1978), available in three editions in the U.S.A. (Donald Grant, illustrated hardback; Walker hardback; Dell paperback) and *Dracula, My Love* (London, 1980) were Tremayne's answer to a Dracula trilogy.

With the Dracula trilogy, Tremayne tried to give women characters a more active role. Tremayne is a feminist and felt that the idea of Dracula could be added to. Whether Tremayne has done this successfully, or not, is left to the quibblers. Tremayne has moved on to different pastures.

Lan Kern is a character that Tremayne developed for a story with Celtic settings. It is a story that is heroic fantasy, rather than horror, and the Lan Kern series is a trilogy.

The Fires of Lan Kern (London, 1980) has been released in the U.S. by St. Martin's Press. *The Destroyers of Lan Kern* and *Buccaneers of Lan Kern* will become available later.

Tremayne says that the theme for Lan Kern, the quest for a magic vessel, goes back to the pre-Christian Welsh myth of "The Spoils of Annwyn." Several Celtic myths and a few Irish myths are used throughout Lan Kern, but only as ideas—not storylines.

Zombie! (London, 1981) is a quiet little book which followed *Dracula, My Love* and preceded *The Return of Raffles* (London, 1981). The cover boasts "the blood-freezing chiller sensation" and is adorned by an ugly old woman holding a blood-dripping dagger.

The story is about a young woman who goes to the Caribbean Islands to search her family roots, because she has been named in a will, and finds the dark side of voodoo. Tremayne's descriptive pen is another example of his creativity in action.

Ten full minutes passed before there was a movement at the door of the bungalow. It creaked open and a figure appeared. It was impossible to tell whether it was male or female. From neck to feet it was covered in a loose robe which seemed to consist of layers of bird feathers, brightly coloured and exotic bird feathers, which rippled and danced in the ·faint morning breeze. On the head, completely covering it, was a hideous mask. It seemed to represent some kind of reptilian face whose features were unimaginable outside of Hades. (p. 2)

Though the majority of the works written by Tremayne are novels, two of the titles are anthologies. *Masters of Terror: William Hope Hodgson* (Corgi, 1977)—the introduction of this book has been published in the British Fantasy Society's centenary tribute pamphlet—and *Irish Masters of Fantasy* (Wolfhound Press, 1979).

Irish Masters of Fantasy, which has provoked mixed feelings from critics here (U.S.), contains biographical essays on Charles Robert Maturin, Joseph Sheridan LeFanu, Fitz-James O'Brien, Bram Stoker, M.P. Shiel, and Lord Dunsany. This book also contains portraits and drawings.

Tremayne's work has received critical acclaim in England as well as in the U.S. "Bloody good...It is indeed a sweet piece of prose..." said *Penthouse* (on *Bloodright*).

"A product of a keen and imaginative mind..." said *Publishers Weekly* of *The Fires of Lan Kern*.

The thing that makes Peter Ellis Tremayne amazing is that while writing as Tremayne, Peter Ellis retained his own established career. Under his own name, Ellis wrote six additional books from 1977-1982, one of which, *The Liberty Tree!* (London, 1982), was a novel.

"A novel of 80,000 words, written at a comfortable pace," Ellis says, "would normally take me ten weeks. That's allowing for two drafts—one written at 'white heat' and the other written for corrections and polishing."

Not only has Ellis written novels and books, and edited anthologies, he has written countless articles, book reviews and short stories. Of his published poetry, *The Empty Glens* was set to music by Greek composer Christos Pittas, who wrote the musical score/setting for Tanith Lee's play (*Bitter Gate*) on BBC radio.

Ellis doesn't feel that he's achieved the status of being a "success."

"Success is a relative term. I don't feel successful as yet and so that is the yardstick used: my own definition."

Currently living in London with his wife, Dorothy, Ellis keeps writing. "Trying to entertain..." he smiles, "and on the way get people thinking...."

Biographical information was obtained from: *Cornish Life, Contemporary Authors* (Vol. 81-84), *Books In Print* (Author Index), *International Authors and Writers Who's Who*, Count Dracula Fan Club and Peter Berresford Ellis.

BIBLIOGRAPHY

The Hound of Frankenstein. Ventura Books, 1977.
Dracula Unborn. Bailey Bros. & Swinfen/Corgi, 1977, Dell, 1979.
Masters of Terror: William Hope Hodgson. Corgi, 1977.
The Vengeance of She. Sphere, 1978.
The Revenge of Dracula. Bailey Bros. & Swinfen, 1978.
The Ants. Sphere, 1979.
Irish Masters of Fantasy. Wolfhound Press, 1979.
The Curse of Loch Ness. Sphere, 1979.
The Fires of Lan Kern. Bailey Bros. & Swinfen, 1980.
Dracula, My Love. Bailey Bros. & Swinfen, 1980.
Zombie! Sphere, 1981.
The Return of Raffles. Magnun Books, 1981.
The Morgow Rises! Sphere, 1982.
The Destroyers of Lan Kern. Bailey Bros. & Swinfen, 1982.

THREE POETS OF HORROR:
TIERNEY, BREIDING, AND BRENNAN
by Steve Eng

"On the gloomy background of the panorama of the world the poetic dreamer rises, gaunt, eyes laden with veiled fires. He stands gestureless, and dominates the world through an omnipotent sixth sense."
—Benjamin De Casseres
Forty Immortals (1926)

I
INTRODUCTION

From the earliest tribal times audiences have taken for granted the weird and horrorific in poetry. Initially, of course, poetry, magic and religion were fused. Later as Christianity spread throughout Western Europe, ghosts and other ethereal entities lived on in ballads and verse dramas, as symbols of the unseen land beyond the barriers of faith and reason.

In fact, elements of the bizarre and uncanny appear in nearly every major poet through Yeats. Usually it is credible achievement, from the ghosts of Shakespeare to the Death-Coach of young Tennyson to Poe's ghoul-haunted woodland of Weir. (The early, bad Gothic poems of Shelley are an exception.)

With this century's modern poetry upheaval, however, horror verse being almost always rhymed and metered, was a casualty. Often shunning religion and reveling in mundane despair, contemporary poets have little use for the daemon lover, the banshee, the graveyard spectre or the malign fairy.

In England fantastic verse died out, there being no successors to poets like Alfred Noyes, Walter de la Mare or John Masefield. In America horror poems were given a shabby but secure shelter for decades in the pulp pages of *Weird Tales* (1923-1954), where verse complemented the stories. Significantly the three premier fictioneers of "The Unique Magazine" were its most prolific, important poets: H.P. Lovecraft, Clark Ashton Smith and Robert E. Howard.

Lovecraft's sonnet sequence, *Fungi From Yuggoth* (written 1929-1930), became very influential in the burgeoning Small Press movement of the late 1960s-1970s. It has the locale of his fiction (Arkham, Innsmouth, etc.) and the pieces are like chapters of a novel—some of them snap shut with decisive endings while others are more evocative; generally they impel the reader forward. The *Fungi* are a *tour de force*, though some are melodramatic due to their brevity. The sonnets can also stand separately and are sometimes published singly. Beginning horror poets often slavishly imitate them, aping Lovecraft's diction and mood, his gods and New England region and of course his rhyme scheme (the octet is often Petrarchan with varying sestets but always climaxed by a couplet). Today it is called the "Lovecraftian" sonnet though the form can be found in Dante Rossetti, and even Sir Thomas Wyatt of the early sixteenth century. The greatest shortcoming is the final two lines which tend toward a double-pitch surprise ending, or an all-too-predictable one. Lovecraft saw his sonnets as a continuum, where even the more explosive ones are a part of a whole (and also, relating to his fiction). His successors, too often, write their sonnets as ends in themselves, resulting sometimes in overly sensational little horror tales in verse.

Another tradition was set in motion by Lovecraft's friend Clark Ashton Smith, that of lush romantic verse rich in lapidary rhetoric and cold remoteness. Archaic in vocabulary like no poetry in English, the work of Smith suggests Swinburne's heavier music, Coleridge's imagination and Baudelaire's decadence. Add the mockery of Ambrose Bierce and the cosmicism of George Sterling and there emerges the monumental Smith of the posthumous *Selected Poems* (1971). Like Lovecraft's *Fungi*, the poetry of Smith has had a pervasive effect and not always a benign one. Smith is rather static and descriptive, and imitators cannot approach his sense of language.

Less influential is the skilled, highly popular Robert E. Howard whose poetic subjects are at least as bleak as those of Lovecraft and Smith. His black philosophy and despair particularly ally him with modern verse of the weird. But his violent, sword-and-sorcery cadence is too dynamic for the average apprentice poet to copy; he has few imitators.

II
RICHARD L. TIERNEY: ARCANE SONNETEER

Each of these three poets has left a deep mark upon the work of Richard L. Tierney, whose horror poetry spans a decade and a half since the days of *The Arkham Collector*. Born in 1936, Tierney has lived most of his life in the Midwest (Iowa and Minnesota). When he was very young his grandmother read him Poe, and in high school he discovered August Derleth's landmark anthology, *Dark of the Moon: Poems of Fantasy and the Macabre* (1947) and as he says (letter 6 September 1983) "...practically memorized it. The poems in it that really gripped me were Lovecraft's *Fungi from Yuggoth*, Clark Ashton Smith's "The Hashish-Eater" and James Thompson's "The City of Dreadful Night.""

Tierney's education was in entomology, not actually surprising considering the tendency for romantic writers to pursue scientific interests.[1] For many years Tierney has worked as a forest ranger, also spending some time with an occult publisher; of late he has co-authored (with David C. Smith) numerous Robert E. Howard continuations (*Red Sonja* series).

Even as Tierney was inclining toward horror poetry, August Derleth of Arkham House was lamenting in 1961 how the genre was dwindling. In his anthology *Fire and Sleet and Candlelight: New Poems of the Macabre* he noticed recent poets' "extreme preoccupation with themselves" (p. xix) turning them away from the fantastic. Later in the decade Derleth's *Arkham Collector* was publishing new horror poetry, including Tierney's. In the 1970s Tierney's reputation had been made chiefly by his Lovecraftian sonnets, and by 1981 his *Collected Poems* included forty-four sonnets varying in form, and in literary inspiration. No less that forty owe to Lovecraft in their rhyme scheme, and their usually familiar themes bid for the reader's attention. They amply illustrate the opportunities and risks of the *Fungi* tradition. The paramount challenge is how to resolve the sonnet with a sense of finality and not jerking melodrama; the stateliness of sonnets generally rather demands a muted closing. This is especially vital when the poem stands alone, as most of Tierney's do.

In "The Pinnacles" (in *Collected Poems*) Tierney nimbly sidesteps the Lovecraftian pitfalls:

Against the twilight I have seen them rise—
Those high thin spires, forbidding and immense,
Like broken fangs or shattered battlements,
Piercing the cloudless blue of desert skies.
Sometimes I seem to feel their watching eyes
When I draw near, and always I grow tense
As if somehow their contours let me sense
Some vast and evil thing that never dies.

What waits and broods beneath these looming cliffs
I do not know, but sometimes I can trace
The dim remains of monstrous hieroglyphs
Where sunsets limn the cliff's basaltic face,
While often deep in dreams I catch the sound
Of ponderous footsteps far beneath the ground. (p. 25)

The tone is soft, like Lovecraft at his more restrained (as in *Fungi* XXIII, XXX, XXVI and especially XXVIII, "Expectancy").[2] The first

horrorific word encountered in "The Pinnacles" is "forbidding" followed
by "broken fangs," but then a restrained tension is sustained till "vast
and evil thing" so that the coming horror is more effective, the way
being prepared by ethereal lyricism. Also, the final couplet does not
close with a click—the poet only dreams "I catch the sound"; and the
rounded "ponderous" besides echoing the previous vowels, makes "footsteps" seem less emphatic. It should be noted how vowels are elsewhere used for sonorous, grand effects ("broods"..."looming"), and how
the earlier consonance of "shattered battlements" offsets some of the
gentleness. Tierney has the kind of ear common to the late Victorians,
so such romantic tricks of the craft are commonplace in his work. The
understated horror in the final couplet conveys *unease*, not shock,
unlike many poems emulating Lovecraft.

"The Pinnacles" also has an unearthly sense of locale. Other
Tierney poems have an even sharper feel for place, such as "The Vol-
cano" which captures the tropic terror of Mount Pelee's eruption
(heightened by the presence of hellish Shapes). Others range from the
frozen North ("The Sleeper") to bleak deserts ("The Legend," "The Pil-
grimage," "Yahweh") to the fantasy realms of Lovecraft ("Mountains of
Madness") and Robert W. Chambers ("Carcosa"). Tierney distinguishes
himself from the lesser fantasy poets who might merely drop place
names and stock geographic descriptions into their poems: his feel for
place in authentic. One of his hobbies is archaeology. Over four
winters (1963-1966) he visited ancient Indian sites in Latin America,
climbing an Honduran pyramid to recite aloud poems from Frank
Belknap Long's *In Mayan Splendor*; and in the late 1960s near Napa,
California, he managed to salvage some relics from an Indian village
about to be bulldozed. The archaeological spirit infuses the sonnet
"Tahuantin-Suyu" which, though not horrific, hurls both the place and
the time of the ancient Incas defiantly at our mediocre modern age.
Tierney's hatred of the present recalls Smith and Lovecraft. He cap-
tures another remote setting in "The Wendigo" sonnet, after Algernon
Blackwood's famous tale.

Tierney in this poem also handles the malign presence subtly in
the sestet:

> Now as the twilight fades to deeper gloom
> A glowing shadow glides among the trees;
> The forest knows the stillness of the tomb,
> And then—what eerie, half-heard tones are these
> That echo strangely over lake and pond,
> Luring the listener to the vast beyond? (p. 52)

In the couplet Tierney resists the tempting climax of having the
Wendigo descend, wings a-flap, as a lesser poet might have done.
Like Blackwood's story, the effect is the more unsettling for its indi-

rectedness. Tierney similarly resolves "The Swamp Dweller" sonnet: instead of releasing a marsh-creature with shocking force in the terminal couplet, his monster will merely "softly rise to stalk the silent woods" (p. 55). There are some less successful examples, more obvious in their effects, suggesting Tierney might usefully try the Petrarchan sonnet more often, with its subtler octet (rhyming *cdecde*, etc.); and his "doom/tomb/gloom" type rhymes could be avoided.

Recently in *The Twilight Zone Magazine* 2, No. 2 (May 1982) Tierney received more space than perhaps any living fantasy poet has in a newsstand publication—seven of his poems appeared. Nearly all of these deal with our modern, very-near future horror of nuclear death. Here Tierney is closely allied with that friend of Sterling and Smith, Californian Stanton A. Coblentz, who railed against war in a similar, late Victorian style. Tierney exceeds Coblentz in ferocious rage. "The Great City" recalls how the American Indian once held the land in respectful stewardship, till it was seized and ruined by the more barbaric white people. To Tierney, nuclear death for America is only just deserts. Here, the climactic couplet is an asset and the heavy emphasis is not wrong: "And monstrous fires atomic shall congeal/The sundered atoms of your glass and steel" (p. 62). His ironically titled "Optimism" makes a similar point: Man is devolving toward final, suicidal savagery. Tierney cannot wait till when "O'er the red horizon high and proud/Expand the billows of a mushroom cloud" (p. 63). A brazen cruelty reminiscent of Robert E. Howard fires this anti-war poem into more intensity than is usual for protest verse. Its mocking iconoclasm is uncompromising; such amused fury is more telling than the solemnity of the conventional Armageddon poem.

Tierney has a seeming atheistic contempt for ant-like Man, and for the feeble God of those preachers who cannot see beyond the bridge of their noses to the nuclear fate that our Christian nation has pioneered. Actually, this sharp irreverence is more pious than many a cautious church sermon about "peace." (Tierney doubtless enjoyed the TV drama *The Day After* in 1983, with its radiation-silhouettes of skeletons!)

Tierney brightens occasional poems with the welcome presence of women, sometimes veiled and unreal, sometimes invitingly carnal. "Fulfillment," in tercets, is sensuous in Tierney's typical *fin de siecle* tone with the cruelty of a femme fatale, whom the poet loves with the assistance of marijuana. Similarly decadent are some of Baudelaire's *Les Fleurs du Mal* he has translated, such as the erotic and weird "The Giantess" (done in shorter, pentameter feet than Clark Ashton Smith's Alexandrine version).

The poet also echoes the pitch-dark rebelliousness of Robert E. Howard in such poems as "Hate" with its elegiac quatrains striking harder than is usual for the form (popularized by Thomas Gray for his tranquil churchyard):

> If hate were water I would be a well
>   Whose depth no line could sound, no light illume,
> And from my source, warmed by the fires of hell,
>   Would gush a flood of universal doom.
>
> If hate were flame, then at my fierce commands
>   The fires within the earth would seethe and rise,
> Shatter the crust and flood the quaking lands,
>   Rolling the smoke of doom against the skies.
>
> But hate is hate, and I am but a man
>   Trapped on a line of history's hackneyed page,
> Restrained by human chains and therefore can
>   But gnaw my soul in black impotent rage. (p. 15)

Such passionate anger is somewhat refreshing in an age where poets too often turn hostility inward, making dulled, depressed poetry. Some might find Tierney's tone forced and strident however.

Thus in various forms, sonnets predominating, Tierney writes primarily of horror set against historical and literary backdrops, looking ahead at times into the abyss of Armageddon. His poems exemplify the potentials and risks of coping with the immediate literary tradition of *Weird Tales* and its Victorian antecedents. Tierney however, interestingly brings a softer musical gift not found in his models, and his blacker themes do not give it full release. His supple supple skill could achieve different results than those of his mentors Lovecraft, Smith, and Howard. The fantasy field (and especially the horror genre) tends to reward obvious, recognizable work, so the incentive for Tierney to develop may not be strong. He is meanwhile preoccupied with fiction. His *Collected Poems* have crystalized his muse, but some enterprising, smaller firm should commission a shorter Tierney volume on different themes to launch his next period.

III
G. SUTTON BREIDING: SAN FRANCISCO SURREALIST

A major fantasy journal is *Nyctalops*, which since 1970 has been evolving beyond a mere Lovecraftian format, to a mood more surreal and modern. Tierney has frequently appeared in its pages; so too has G. Sutton Breiding. Born in 1950 in West Virginia, Breiding today is an office worker in San Francisco. He began writing at age fourteen, and in a Catholic high school outraged his teachers with his first newsletter. His numerous amateur journals have more recently

144

drawn offended comment from readers, in keeping with his homage to such decadent heroes as Baudelaire and Rimbaud.

Despite living in the city of Bierce and George Sterling, with its Clark Ashton Smith associations, Breiding depends less than Tierney upon the recent weird poetry tradition. While his language remains late romantic like Tierney's, he has a more modern tone and form (being mostly free verse). He has grown toward this modernity; earlier, he worked more often within fixed measures, such as in "Fables" an earlier poem reprinted in his first collection *Autumn Roses* (1984), where "Black Pegasus flies swiftly through my songs" and in the final stanza:

> My laughter is entombed in nameless grief;
> My flutes are crushed and shattered in the mud;
> A baleful, frantic music is in the phantom hills:
> Foreboding centaurs' bones, and nymphs' degraded
> blood. (p. 8)

The cadence is elegiac, but the music and perversity are Eighteen Nineties. Of similar vintage in inspiration is "Song of the Sirens" in the same volume. There have been many poems of this or similar title, but Breiding's is novel since narrated by the siren herself. The lyrical grace is weighted down by the grim intent of the siren, as in the second stanza:

> Beneath the waves of liquid jade
> Return to what your dreams have made:
> In coral kingdoms dreams are found
> And you will find your heart has drowned
> Where the bones of fallen dreams are laid. (p. 12)

She sings with further malignancy in the last three lines of the next stanzas: "Where the tongues of poets come to sleep,/And sailors' hearts are mine to reap;/Where restless singers' dooms are spun." Through this poem the lapping waves are evoked by the cinquain form, and the tetrameter length is right.

Since he mostly writes free verse, Breiding allows the contemporary, less rhythmic line to provide tension between romantic rhetorical content and modern form. He writes prose poetry as well, in the vein of Baudelaire or Clark Ashton Smith. Copious amounts of his work are found in the ephemeral pages of the several magazines he has edited (e.g., *Black Wolf*, *The Punk Surrealist Cafe*, *A Clerk's Journal*, *Folklore*, or *Starfire* edited by his brother Bill Breiding). The outre subjects and surrealistic style have probably influenced *Nyctalops*, and partly Thomas Wiloch's *Grimoire* which derives even more directly from the mainstream *Kayak*. *Grimoire* features Breiding and others of his school.

Breiding typically strikes the fashionable depressed note of the moderns, nonetheless sincerely, striving for the startling image but retaining the colored adjectives of aesthetes like Clark Ashton Smith. The combination is uniquely his own. He is the most modern of those California romantics so often commemorated by Donald Sidney-Fryer (who appropriately introduces Breiding's *Autumn Roses*.)

His erotic frankness, like Tierney's, by its very existence is healthy, in a field where stifled sexuality seems almost a convention. Carnal audacity is one of Breiding's trademarks. A characteristic effort in *Autumn Roses* is "Entreaty" which ends:

> O Queen of the marbled night
> Whose moonlit breasts like seawaves
> Rise and fall in gentle, fevered rhythms—
> Work a necromantic charm
> To carry me, deliver me from Earth,
> Into the far ensorcelled regions
> Of your lovely, monstrous heart. (p. 2)

A similar, perhaps more arresting verse is "Mannequin" (*The Punk Surrealist Cafe* No. 5, 1981), whose jarring first line sets the tone: "Out of the inferno of your flesh/Rise screaming golden harpies/Into the steaming nights of myth" (p. 5). There are modern images of "sweating, perpetual motion machines" that emit "chrome shrieks," juxtaposed with "snarling contortions of pteranodons/Writhing in the swamps/Of scarlet, prehistoric twilights." The chilling close of the poem sounds with the

> roar of black Antarctic winds
> And of haunted werewolves passing
> Through blue and hollow caverns
> Of your immemorial skull. (p. 5)

Breiding has an alert ear for the desolate, haunting image— "in the sovereign tombs of the centuries/that the fugitive heart calls/home"—or "autumn-blooming roses/and lilies carved of ice"—and in "No Investigation" (*The Punk Surrealist Cafe* No. 4, 1981) there are numerous quotable lines: "I am remembered/Only by your ghosts"..."your thin red lips/Performing cruelties in the turquoise air"..."I am the yellow sigh of dead lives/A stick man bent in the hurried wind/Putrescent with spent lives..A detective of misery..." (p. 12).

The poet is rarely topical, but there are two outstanding exceptions. One is "San Francisco" (*Autumn Roses*), an exquisite evocation of a city that is usually romanticized ecstatically. From Breiding's pen the Bay City is:

>secret maze of
>lost & tangled streets
>your haunted nameless monuments
>that stand like signals
>from another world. (p. 16)

where there is "ragged lace hanging/in the windows of decrepit/gabled towers." The contemporary scene is deplored, being "filled with drunken zombies" and "modern vampires." Certainly not a Chamber of Commerce piece to boost tourism!—but the poem is a link between George Sterling and Allen Ginsberg, though written around twenty years after the Beat poetry movement.

The other topical verse is "Necrophiliac's Manifesto" (1981 leaflet) which, despite its title, is not a satire but an ironic tribute to departed romantics—Poe, Baudelaire, Smith and Sterling among others, "garret-ghosts and absinthe drinkers." Breiding affects to not mourn for them since they are disembodied creatures with no ties to our modern age: "only golden typewriters will record their amnesias." Then he admits he really worships them, for:

>The dead give birth to the dead.
>By imagining that I am alive
>I can dream my way
>Back to the grave.

Breiding's gift for language manages to fuse aesthetic lushness to sometimes violent modern images. Sterling and Smith have a falling, passive sound; so does Breiding till he counters it with his own violence and humor. The effect is rather that of Clark Ashton Smith enjoying espresso coffee with the North Beach Beats of the 1950s. As for topics, Breiding relies mostly on literary or personal decadence and this runs the hazard of monotony. That is the fallacy of romanticism generally, perpetually squeezing one's own soul for material because traditions (and Establishments) have grown stale. Self-pity is already endemic to romantic poets, and it threatens to become *the* subject when inspiration fails. Not drawn to narrative poetry nor to its typical folklore themes, Breiding might wisely begin creating a recognizable poetic mythology with interlocking themes and symbols. Romantics, when they don't die young, often become bored with their own reiterated pains and madness, and simply cease to write. The problem of renewal and development will confront Breiding at some point.

Meanwhile, Sutton Breiding may be the most arresting figure of a disturbing surrealist poetry movement. In his hands the distortions and *non sequiturs* make crazy sense. Because he couches his horrors garishly in romantic metaphor, his modern panic is memorable. Nor is he boring, which cannot be said of so many of the thousands of super-serious modern poets who have affected (from a safe distance) the kind of perilous decadence Breiding exults in up close. He remarks (letter, 30 September 1983):

> I am eternally in search of Beauty—the fatal and there-
> fore vital force and allure of Romance. I am a cynical
> Romantic, doomsayer, morose nihilist—yet I will search
> the tomb for my final ecstasy.

Elsewhere he frequently tosses out epigrammatic manifestoes about his art, as in *Black Wolf* No. 10 (August 1974):

> I fling words haphazardly, petulantly, desperately in
> search of phantom treasure...Moonlight shadows the
> roots of my verse...My lute is cut from onyx: my violin
> black with the mouldering bones of Zann. My Muse,
> Faire Succubus, horned with Night & Death, The
> Darkest of Roses, demands insanity to the hilt like the
> driven daggers of Love. All my songs are Lunes to the
> most beautiful of all moons: the one that rises above
> the fretted towers of Atlantis, & Arkham's brooding
> graveyards... (p. 1)

Whether Breiding is wholly serious is unimportant, since the mystique of his poetry creates its own sincerity even though sometimes we smile, half-sensing Breiding is laughing too.

Where poetry ends and posture begins is not always clear but the lyrical language and grim perspective might define Breiding as a romantic existentialist.

IV
JOSEPH PAYNE BRENNAN: BARD OF BLACK DECEMBERS

The most established horror poet is the prolific Joseph Payne Brennan, even better known for his weird and detective fiction. Born in 1918 in Connecticut, Brennan has worked for over forty years at the Yale University Library. He sold his first poem in 1940, and since the 1950s much of his work has been in non-fantasy verse (he edited the poetry journal *Essence*, 1950-1977). Despite appearances in prestige journals and numerous anthologies, Brennan has understandably made a deeper impression upon the fantasy field. This is because the genre still provides a poet with readers other than fellow poets and critics. As Brennan comments (letter, 9 October 1983): "Mainstream poetry in

America seems to have passed into the almost exclusive control of college English teachers."

Despite writing mostly free verse which is the fashion today, Brennan is distanced from his contemporaries in various ways. One distinction is his supernatural subject matter "at which the academics often shrug, if not sneer!" Another is his preference for clarity and logical sequence; he does not subscribe to the theory that modern life is chaotic, and so should be the form of poetry, believing instead that "the poem, not the reader, should do most of the work. If it doesn't *communicate*, it is a trash heap of words."

Also Brennan's evocations of Nature are rather traditional. His non-fantasy poems often deal with the outdoors, and so do enough of his horror verses that he might be termed a decadent Nature poet. (Up to the age of fourteen he spent at least three months each year on his grandmother's farm.) In his first fantasy verse collection, *Nightmare Need* (1964), around half the selections have rural or seasonal elements, and this ratio would seem to obtain in his later output.

Like Thomas Hardy, Brennan prefers the end of the year, poetically. "Judgement Day" in *Edges of Night* (1974) begins:

I dreamed I watched the wet October wind
whirling its leaves past the skeleton stones;
I conjured up the corps of coffined dead,
scaled in their runnelled sockets like a crop. (p. 11)

And in "Pasture Silence" (*Edges of Night*) he asserts that New England pastures "pummeled by autumn,/summon up a marrow-deep melancholy/nothing else evokes" (p.43). In "Halloween Snow" in *Creep to Death* (1982) the handfuls of snow are frozen confetti" (p. 46) and the cornstalks seem to whisper in the cold, appearing as "rows of desiccated witches." In the same volume "Gradations of Death" has gravestones scraped by autumn leaves.

Born in December, Brennan hangs many of his poems with the icicles of Death. In "The Trail I Took" (*Creep to Death*) there are "The hatchet winds of hag December" (p. 113), a poem where the narrator reports his own drowning. As he suggests in "The Snow Wish" (*Nightmare Need*) "We dream of sleep and dark returnings,/We would escape to a magic wood of snow" (p. 19). "Demons' Wood" in *A Sheaf of Snow Poems* (1973) similarly states: "In fevered sleep I sought the snow/Deep in a wood the demons know" (p. 12). Throughout his books Brennan's formula of Death=Winter recurs, as in "The Wind of Time" (*Nightmare Need*) where the memory searches out a vanished love:

In some haunted winter room
Her still white face awaits me yet;

Her gothic gift and her impassive grace
Stain the towering darkness like a star. (p. 54)

As Brennan acknowledges in an interview in *Threshold of Fantasy* No.
1 (Spring 1982): "Main themes of my poetry seem to be death, loss, the
mystery of time, Nature" (p. 13), and he might have added: many of
his verses combine all of those themes.

He observes also: "Short stories *narrate*; poems establish a
theme, a mood, a concept—or perhaps merely describe. That's over-
simplifying, of course. A good short story shares some of the functions of a poem—mood, concentrated emotion, etc." Indeed, several of
Brennan's poems are eerie little tales, where just enough "happens" but
not too much (unlike the typical novice's horror poem with the melodramatic conclusion). The reader feels he is allowed to peer beyond
and glimpse something elusive and weird, like "The White Huntress"
(*Nightmare Need*) who:

Never grows weary.
Her swift hounds
Race on phantom feet,
Tireless, never swerving. (p. 64)

and at the poem's climax, she even makes the sun go white. (Frosty
white is a favorite "dark" color for Brennan, the frigid hue of Death.)
In "An Hour After Midnight" (*Nightmare Need*) monsters emerge
from manhole covers and sewers—but the denouement is superbly understated: "When morning broke,/Not a soul came out of the
houses,/Not one." (p. 27)

One of Brennan's stories in verse indulges his too-seldom-heard
wit, "False Humor" in *Webs of Time* (1979)—a B-movie mad scientist
with a "secret ray" resurrects the dead, and onlooking crowds think it
is the Second Coming. When the scientist snaps off his ray and the
dead return graveward, the incensed spectators go crazy and savage the
scientist physically.

One might expect Brennan, as storyteller in verse, to hark back
to the old ballad tradition. He has a stated interest in researching the
Irish sept, the Brennans of Kilkenny, dispossessed by the Earl of
Strafford; one thinks too of the old highwayman ballad, "Brennan on
the Moor." One of his early efforts in "The Last Pagan Mourns for
Dark Rosaleen" in August Derleth, ed., *Fire and Sleet and Candlelight:
New Poems of the Macabre* (1961) a splendid Celtic lament with lines
like "Who has doubted my Dark Rosaleen/Dreams of the grave?/Of the
cairn-littered grave?" (p. 36). But, unlike earlier Arkham House poet
Leah Bodine Drake, Brennan seems to have moved out of the ballad
mode.

150

He stands fairly apart from past fantasy poetry traditions, though paradoxically he is severely obsessed by Time. He attributes this to the destruction of old New Haven, in the *Threshold of Fantasy* interview: "I began to feel that as the city was destroyed, I myself was being partly destroyed along with it" (p. 12) and in a letter (6 February 1984) "The senseless destruction of old buildings makes me almost physically ill...four-fifths of old New Haven has been smashed away." He has written of this in "My Ghosts of Old New Haven," an essay in the program book for World Fantasy Convention '82. Of course, fantasy authors are often preoccupied with Time's leveling of the past; Lovecraft is the most obvious example (his poem "Brick Row" about demolished Providence buildings coming to mind[3]). In *Nightmare Need*, "On Desolate Streets" exploits this mood:

I have wandered on desolate streets
Crying for time to turn back,
Seeking a vanished face, a forgotten door,
Hungry as a famished ghost . . . (p. 36)

And in the same volume Time's cruelty toward lost love is raised to hyperbolic horror in "Epitaph" where the narrator cries: "Knowing it was her,/I could lift the sunken skull,/And kiss its vacant mouth" (p. 39), a *tour de force* poem this writer has re-read many times in over fifteen years.

The ultimate meaning of Time to a poet like Brennan, of course, is its terminus in Death. In "Refrain" (*Creep to Death*) he says it has been whispering in his ears for fifty years which we almost disbelieve—but for his rather unbroken poetic malaise across the decades confirming it. He does not healthily mock Death like the Jacobeans, or attempt to cope with it like Thomas Lovell Beddoes. Brennan merely hammers on its inevitability from many angles (destruction of buildings, lost and deceased love, dire December, etc.), but in the same mood. In "The Dead Reach Out" (*Nightmare Need*) he listens to those departed souls who beseech: "Avenge us! Mark our names! Remember us!" Often in his verse Brennan presses the point that Death wipes even memory out, that no one is much likely to remember us after our last departure.

Surprisingly, Brennan's father died with that not-unusual ecstasy often noticed by those in attendance at death-beds. The poet records this in "My Father's Death" (*Creep to Death*), and echoes it hopefully in "Where in Blinding Light" within the same collection. For him, rare optimism!

With supernatural horror and Death itself omnipresent, Brennan understandably explores a little psychological horror as well. He mentions in "The Cold Corridors" (*Nightmare Need*) that "the mind hoards phantoms." Elsewhere he writes some first-person, chiller poems of madness.

In the area of technique Brennan's penchant for free verse has been mentioned. It arises not out of laziness, or ineptness with fixed forms. He writes adequate metric verse when he chooses, though seemingly not in the sonnet mode nor in blank verse such as Clark Ashton Smith at times employed. Here again, in occasionally handling metrics, he differs from so many contemporaries who have no skill at formal prosody. His brevity is also somewhat traditional, recalling Emily Dickinson, Houseman or Hardy. Introducing *Webs of Time*, Frederick J. Mayer writes: "Brennan is a master of the short poem...brief, concentrated—and often unpredictable until the last line" (p. 2).

Also, with the professionalism of the fiction writer, he pushes poems to conclusion giving aesthetic pleasure from the sense of completeness (though he rarely resorts to italics or exclamation points like poets overly influenced by the pulp magazines). As he comments (letter, 9 October 1983):

> A poem should not merely *incline*; it should at least tend to *compel*. Reams of chopped-up prose pass as poetry today. Poetry need not rhyme, nor even scan with precision, but it should have a *compression and intensity which most prose rarely achieves*. Merely to string out broken lines on a page and call it poetry will not pass (at least not for long).

Brennan's verse is nearly always poetry, stripped as it is of excess, and seemingly written out of emotional necessity. There is, thankfully, none of the idle regional poetaster in him, writing Nature verses on cue for provincial acclaim. Happily (if that is the word) he has bent his mainstream skills and New Englander's eye for the out-of-doors to the needs of the horror field. His prose-writing discipline has given him considerable control and polish as poet.[4]

Meanwhile accolades like the first International Clark Ashton Smith Poet Award (for Outstanding Achievement, a lifetime award), and the Balrog, are tangible recognition. As early as 1961 Brennan had more entries that any other poet in Derleth's *Fire and Sleet and Candlelight: New Poems of Macabre*—fourteen. On the dust-wrapper of *Creep to Death* Derleth is quoted:

> Brennan is not adequately appreciated as a poet in America...he is that kind of poet who may well be read years from now when the considerably more publicized

among his contemporaries have been relegated to a relatively unimportant niche in American literary history.

In the horror field he has had small books of verse and one spacious, luxury edition with illustrations. Brennan now needs a compact, standard volume, like Clark Ashton Smith's *Selected Poems*, but the prospects are faint. At least Brennan has followed Tierney with a prestigious appearance in *Twilight Zone* magazine—his poems were featured with illustrations in a seven-page spread in the June 1984 issue. This is probably the largest such periodical coverage in the history of the genre.

V
CONCLUSION

Whatever the adversities facing poets generally, it is fortunate that by the 1980s Tierney, Breiding and Brennan have persevered against the odds in the horror field to win actual readers. None had taken the comfortable, institutional route, and each has hurdled some personal obstacles and plain ill luck. At their best, they have achieved work of high quality within the genre and, importantly, poetry that is interesting in a willful, bizarre way. The narrow range and near-unremitting grimness can be found against all three poets. The charge that over-riding preoccupation with Death and the dark fantastic is adolescent is familiar—is mildly justified—and is mostly irrelevant. Horror poems like their short story counterparts are best not read all at once, and are partaken for enjoyment of the deeper kind that cuts through the civilized crust of consciousness. Whether an old ghost ballad, or a more modern effort, the poetry of horror if it plumbs the primal depths of fear has done its work. The psychologist or rationalist critic who would point out the infantile source of fear be damned! It is probably *more* immature to deny our basic haunted heritage anyway. It is enough to demand that the bard avoid the cliche, the trite rhyme and the borrowed diction of his predecessors. These three practitioners have already left their mark on the horror genre.

In their wake comes a small legion of other poets and versifiers in the Small Press field also making themselves heard in a unique literary movement. They are the necessary, inevitable allies of the swelling horde of horror fiction writers. The best of them may well make their place with the three poets just discussed. In the words of Robert E. Howard ("The Song of A Mad Minstrel"), they "come with hideous spells, black chants and ghastly tunes."

NOTES

1. Shelley's countless scientific (and pseudo-scientific) experiments, that form the background of his wife's *Frankenstein*, Poe's dabblings, Tennyson's astronomic interest, are only a few examples.
2. One of Lovecraft's literary values was that sense of "adventurous expectancy" he felt at sunsets and other times.
3. Speaking of "Brick Row" in *Lovecraft: A Biography* (1975) L. Sprague de Camp says "Lovecraft's hostility to change was indiscriminate. He would have kept every building built before, say, 1830" (p. 317). Lovecraft is a Brennan favorite, though not a stylistic influence in either prose or verse. (In the 1950s, Brennan published two pioneering scholarly booklets on Lovecraft.)
4. Brennan has introduced the work of two fantasy poets also, Fred C. Adams' *A Bagwyn's Dozen* (1974) and Mary Elizabeth Counselman's *The Face of Fear and Other Poems* (1984).

SOURCES

Portions of this essay first appeared within book reviews—of Richard L. Tierney in Harry O. Morris's *Nyctalops* and of Joseph Payne Brennan in Neil Barron's *Science Fiction & Fantasy Book Review*. Our thanks to those editors.

Breiding, G. Sutton. *Autumn Roses: Selected Poems*. Albuquerque: Silver Scarab Press, 1984.

_____. *The Crosses of December (After Reading George Trakl)*. Madison, WI: The Strange Company, 1977.

Brennan, Joseph Payne. *A Sheaf of Snow Poems*. Hamden, CT: Pendulum Press, 1973.

_____. *As Evening Advances*. Huntsville, AL: Crystal Visions Press, 1978,

_____. *Creep to Death*. West Kensington, RI: Donald M. Grant, 1981.

_____. *Death Poems*. Grand Rapids, MI: Pilot Press Books, 1974.

_____. *Edges of Night*. Grand Rapids, MI: Pilot Press Books, 1974.

_____. "Joseph Payne Brennan in Brief: An Autobiography."
August Derleth Society Newsletter, 2, No. 1 (1978), pp. 6-7.

_____. *Nightmare Need*. Sauk City, WI: Arkham House, 1964.

_____. *Sixty Selected Poems*. Amherst, NY: The New Establishment Press, 1985.

_____. *Webs of Time*. New Haven, CT: Macabre House, 1979.
Eng, Steve. "August Derleth: Friend of Fantasy Poetry." Unpublished bibliographical essay.

_____. "The Poetry of Fantasy: An Essay in Research and Collection." Paper given at The Second Conference on the Fantastic, Boca Raton, 1981.

_____. "Fantasy Genre Poetry" in Frank Magill, ed. *A Survey of Modern Fantasy*. Vol. V. Englewood Cliffs, NJ: Salem Press, 1983, pp. 2415-2421.

_____. "Supernatural Verse in English" in Marshall Tymn, Ed.
Horror Literature: A Core Collection and Reference Guide. New York and London: R.R. Bowker, 1981, pp. 401-452

Grant, Donald M. "Joseph Payne Brennan: Quiet Achiever." *World Fantasy Convention '82* program book, pp. 36-37.

Larson, Randall. "Joseph Payne Brennan: Old Cities and The Stream of Time (interview)." *Threshold of Fantasy: A Magazine of Fantastic Literature* No. 1 (Spring 1982), pp. 4-13.

Tierney, Richard L. *Collected Poems: Nightmares and Visisons*.
Sauk City, WI: Arkham House, 1981 (incorporating *Dreams and Damnations*, 1975).

CONTRIBUTORS

DARRELL SCHWEITZER is the author of three novels, *We Are All Legends, The Shattered Goddess*, and *The White Isle*. His short fiction has appeared in numerous periodicals, including *Twilight Zone, Night Cry, Whispers, Fantastic*, and others; some of it was collected in *Tom O'Bedlam's Night Out and Other Strange Excursions* (1985). He has written critical studies of H.P. Lovecraft, Robert E. Howard, and Lord Dunsany; conducted numerous author interviews, some of which are collected in the *SF Voices* series (Borgo Press); been assistant editor of *Isaac Asimov's Science Fiction Magazine* and later *Amazing*; and is presently a partner in Owlswick Literary Agency and co-editor of the revived *Weird Tales*. He is collaborating with Joel Rosenberg on *Writing Fantasy* for New American Library. He has edited four previous critical symposia: *Discovering Modern Horror Fiction I, Discovering Stephen King, Discovering H.P. Lovecraft*, and *Exploring Fantasy Worlds*.

BERNADETTE BOSKY's essays have been published widely. *Modern Horror* readers will be particularly interested in her careful analysis of the relationship between Stephen King and Peter Straub, which appears in *Discovering Stephen King*, and in her contribution to Underwood and Miller's *Kingdom of Fear, The World of Stephen King*.

MICHAEL E. STAMM was born in Colorado in 1953, and has lived in nine states and in Japan. He has two degrees in History from the University of Oregon, where he now works as Graduate and Composition Secretary for the English Department. He lives in Eugene with his wife, a specialist in education and a teacher of Chinese, and two very strange cats. He has been reviewing books for *Science Fiction and Fantasy Book Review* since 1979, and has also written for *Fantasy Newsletter*. His first love is horror fiction, and some day he hopes to write at least one of the great American horror novels. His essay on Dennis Etchison appears in *Discovering Modern Horror Fiction I*.

GARY WILLIAM CRAWFORD is the editor of the excellent, recently revived scholarly periodical, *Gothic*. He holds an M.A. in English from Mississippi State University. He has published essays on Le Fanu, Ramsey Campbell, and Joyce Carol Oates, and has also written an his-

torical essay and compiled an annotated bibliography of horror literature from 1920 to 1980, published in *Horror Literature* (Bowker, 1981).
His fiction has appeared in *Dark Horizons, Fantasy Tales, Weirdbook,*
and elsewhere.

RANDALL D. LARSON publishes *Threshold of Fantasy* and is also a
Robert Bloch expert, having published *The Robert Bloch Fanzine* in
1972/73, which included a bibliography and essays on Bloch. He has
written *The Reader's Guide to Robert Bloch* for the Starmont series.

JEFFREY K. GODDIN'S short fiction has appeared in *Twilight Zone.*
He is a rare book dealer, formerly an assistant in the Louisville University Library's rare books department, and has published numerous
critical and scholarly essays. His study of Lafcadio Hearn occupied
the entire March 1982 issue of the University of Louisville's *Library
Review,* and is worth seeking out.

DON D'AMMASSA reviews books for *Science Fiction Chronicle* and
publishes the highly-regarded fanzine, *Mythologies.* He has been a
regular essayist in the fantasy/science-fiction field for many years.

T.E.D. KLEIN is an illustrious author of horror fiction in his own
right, and the former editor of *Twilight Zone* magazine. He built a
major reputation on the basis of a mere four stories (for details, see
Robert M. Price's article on him in *Discovering Modern Horror Fiction
I*), which have recently been collected as *Dark Gods.* His first novel,
The Ceremonies (1984), was one of the most eagerly awaited events in
modern horror publishing.

RAMSEY CAMPBELL is another illustrious author, almost too well-
known to require an introduction. There is another article about him,
by Gary Crawford, in *Discovering Modern Fiction I.* Campbell continues to contribute prolifically to the field. Scream Press has recently
announced a collection of his "erotic horror fiction" entitled *Scared
Stiff.*

ALAN WARREN is a freelance writer based in the San Francisco Bay
area. His first story appeared in *Pacific Traveller* when he was 18,
and since then he has written science fiction, suspense, and horror fiction for *Mike Shayne's Mystery Magazine, Isaac Asimov's SF Magazine,* and others, as well as non-fiction for *Film Comment, Cinecurrent,*
and *International Film Buff.* His article on Roald Dahl appears in
Discovering Modern Horror Fiction I. He also has a book on Roald
Dahl coming out from Starmont House.

157

ARTHUR JEAN COX is a specialist in Victoriana, and an author of fantasy fiction, often of antiquarian leanings, including the remarkable "The Collector of Ambroses" (1971). He has written what is perhaps the world's only science-fictional Thackeray pastiche ("A Prince of Snobs," as by Arthur Pendennis, *Amazing*, September 1983). His first story appeared in the *Magazine of Fantasy and Science Fiction* in 1951.

BEN P. INDICK is a playwright, the publisher of *Ibid*, and the author of numerous critical essays which have appeared in all the Schweitzer-edited non-fiction anthologies, and is also in the two Underwood-Miller Stephen King books. He is also the author of *The Drama of Ray Bradbury* (1977).

GILLIAN FITZGERALD is a writer of Irish fantasy, whose work has appeared in *Fantasy and Science Fiction*, *The Dragon*, *Elsewhere*, *The Year's Best Fantasy*, and other places. She considers her interest in vampires to be quite legitimate since she once wrote a horror review column for Marvel Comics' *Tomb of Dracula* entitled, "In a Literary Vein." She is presently at work on a horror novel and an historical fantasy novel.

CHRISTINA KIPLINGER is a writer and poet who hails from Cleveland, Ohio. She has conducted interviews with T.E.D. Klein, Karl Edward Wagner, Dennis Etchison, William F. Nolan, and others. She is a member of SFWA, SPWAO, and Poets & Writers, Inc.

STEVE ENG, who once mentioned that his heart is always stuck in 1890, is one of the editors of that fine periodical *The Romantist*, published by the F. Marion Crawford Society. He is also a poet of considerable note. He has published numerous scholarly articles, mostly on turn-of-the-century fantasy/romantic writers.

INDEX